The River of Life

Andrew E. Terry

Illustrations by Phoebe Terry

TRILOGY CHRISTIAN PUBLISHERS

TUSTIN, CA

Trilogy Christian Publishers
A Wholly Owned Subsidary of Trinity Broadcasting Network
2442 Michelle Drive
Tustin, CA 92780

For information, address Trilogy Christian Publishing

Rights Department, 2442 Michelle Drive, Tustin, Ca 92780.

Trilogy Christian Publishing/ TBN and colophon are trademarks of Trinity Broadcasting Network.

For information about special discounts for bulk purchases, please contact Trilogy Christian Publishing.

Manufactured in the United States of America

Trilogy Disclaimer: The views and content expressed in this book are those of the author and may not necessarily reflect the views and doctrine of Trilogy Christian Publishing or the Trinity Broadcasting Network.

10 9 8 7 6 5 4 3 2 1

Library of Congress Cataloging-in-Publication Data is available.

ISBN 978-1-64773-684-2

ISBN 978-1-64773-685-9 (ebook)

Contents

Dedication

For Phil Leage: to one of the greatest teachers I've ever known. Thank you for always teaching me the importance of application.

For my family. Thank you for all of the color you add every day.

For the encouragers. Never stop; you make the world brighter.

Preface

Many days, whether it's when we lie down or when we wake up—or somewhere in between—we're confronted with thoughts that are contrary to the plans God has for us. They can be thoughts of pride, inadequacy, failure, and/or maybe just a heavy darkness. The longer we entertain those thoughts, the more detailed and dangerous they become. The quicker we can combat those thoughts and replace them with the truth, the better we are. It's never over; it's always a battle.

But the more we have a strategy and we fight, the easier it becomes. So many things can spark one of these thoughts. They can be used to drag us down into a feeling of despair or self-disgust, or to make us think that we are better than everyone around us. However, if we can reach for the One greater than ourselves, it can bring us closer to God and make us more confident in His real purpose for our lives.

Knowing that my life is so vastly different from anyone else's is key. If I live this truth, I won't try to compare my life or my circumstances to anyone else's. Knowing that God has a plan for me unlike any other is paramount to my mental, physical, and spiritual health. Knowing that the plan is not my plan—and that it is in the control of Someone capable of so much more than I am—is one reality I can never get too far away from.

Our lives are like a river, and the path on that river is our own. It intersects with other people—some good, some bad, but all for a reason. I don't need to know every reason for my exact path, but I need to know that there is One who does. He is trustworthy and all-knowing. It's in His hands that I want to abide.

In 2010, I started facilitating groups to read through the Bible in eight days, from Genesis to Revelation. Each morning, I add specific context, history, and other things to look for in the reading for that day. This began because of the immense help the Bible has been in my life—to help me climb out of depression and regain my strength.

Through a series of unfortunate events and the deaths of a few people close to me, I became cynical and pessimistic about most things. Nothing helped, except when I was prompted to read through the Bible in a week. Reluctantly, I did so, and it was the most comprehensive, personal, and timely counseling I could have ever received. It was such an amazing time that a few weeks later, I did it again. I got even more out of it the second time around. I was seeing the big picture of God's plan—how each book fit into the next, and how the whole was a story of love, healing, consequence, real truth, and justice. I felt moved to help other people experience the same thing I had. This book is the result of a lot of struggles and despair that have slowly turned into hope.

This book is about the journey of each one of us, which is unique from everyone else's. In the story, the Holy Spirit is represented by The Guide, and Jesus begins as The Voice, then The Friend, and ends as The Lord. God the Father is represented by The Creator. I took some liberty in exchanging the name Friend (who represents Jesus) for Jesus in some Scriptural references, as noted in the text.

I hope that you will see the relevance and need for this in the story and not jump to the conclusion that it was irreverent. I also hope that you enjoy this book, and that it helps remind you of a perspective greater than your own by the One who is everlasting and loves you more than you'll ever comprehend. Always hope.

ANDREW E. TERRY

CHAPTER 1

Change Will Do You Good

"What we see as only the process of reaching a particular end, God sees as the goal itself."
– Oswald Chambers

It was not every day that Buddy felt like taking a run. He knew it was good for him physically and that it often stimulated his thought process, but it seemed much easier to snuggle up in his cozy bed and drift back into a peaceful sleep. It's just that it felt like so much had been mounting in his life. Relationships that once were fluid now seemed tension-filled; his work that once gave him promise and fulfillment now seemed empty and more meaningless with every passing day. Because all of these things were adding to the unease in his life, everything now seemed more complicated. His problems seemed endless and as though they repetitively circled back to the same situations. Buddy felt a constant stress to do more and be more, which left him unsatisfied.

Buddy had always seen his Decision, three years ago, as the greatest and most life-changing choice of all time. He had wholeheartedly believed that this choice would eventually turn his life around, confirmed by a theory still drifting around in his mind (and even confirmed in the advice of other Seekers) that things would just magically get better. He had thought that all of his current problems in life would be solved and put right immediately, with little effort on his part. He was trying to believe that all that was wrong with his life, relationships, and finances would soon be magically turned from problems to pearls because of that Decision.

His excitement and wishful hoping for this change to take place swiftly had started to turn into a frustration bordering on irritation. After all, he had made that Decision knowing that Jesus paid the price for his sins and for the selfishness in his life that had made it so hard to see God. What a perk that Jesus would take the garbage of his life and turn it around with one simple Decision. If he had known it was that easy, he would not have waited until he was thirty-five to do it.

Unfortunately, in his assessment of the first few years of this new life, not much had changed. The transformation he thought would take place promptly seemed almost nonexistent. Not seeing the desired changes happen had caused those situations and problem areas to increase in complexity and to begin to feel so taxing that he felt like it was it hard to catch a breath sometimes. Buddy's aching heart was so full of disappointment that it seemed to cloud every decision. He had been longing for the freedom and peace that he had read about Jesus bestowing upon those who chose Him. A good long run seemed to help him take a mini vacation from this whole whirlwind that bound him. For some, it was watching a movie or TV show, but for Buddy, temporary freedom came from running.

He was fortunate enough to live in an area that was pleasing to the eye. He lived far enough from town to be "away," but close enough to not spend half his life commuting to work. When he took a run, his usual route took him through the woods and allowed him to wander through a world that seemed exaggeratedly serene. He passed the usual meadow that seemed miles wide. Although it was much prettier in the spring, the summer allowed for a thicker cover that offered amazing privacy. That's what made him feel free on these runs—the privacy and the ability to see no one. Despite the beauty of the surroundings, something seemed monotonous on the run today. He found himself yearning for a different route. Even though the rest of his life seemed like an overbearing challenge, in this case, that's exactly what he was longing for—some challenging terrain, something he could conquer, but most of all, something that he chose, unlike the situations that continually chose him.

Maybe it was this sense of control that he wanted most. So, rather than trotting through the meadow, he decided to make his way through the thicker forest, which provided some rougher, more challenging territory. Maybe he could break a sweat faster, burn some calories, and finally overcome something this week. He ran with an urgency that surprised him. It felt good. Perhaps it was his pace that made the surrounding birch trees blur together into a peaceful white glow. Or perhaps it was something else. It offered him a serenity that he wished he could save, bottle up, and breathe in when life started robbing him of his "fresh air."

Before Buddy knew it, he was into a part of the forest that was totally foreign. Yet he felt safe and familiar, as if he had read about it or heard someone describe it before. Here, the trees provided less cover, and more sun shone through onto the forest floor. It appeared as though the sun was sustaining the environment and reflecting itself in the forest in such a way that it made the ordinary surroundings unique and beautiful. He thought that without the sun's brilliance, this place would be creepy, and even a little frightening.

Suddenly overwhelmed with the magnificence of his surroundings, Buddy stopped to rest on a nearby log, thinking he was on the verge of passing out from running too hard. After all, the environment seemed too magical to be real, so he figured he was about to black out from overexertion.

* * *

As he sat on the log, he felt his heartbeat begin to slow to a steadier pace. But to his amazement, nothing in his surroundings changed; it remained spectacular. As he inspected the log he was sitting on, he saw that someone had been there before. He heard a Voice say,

"Look on the back of the log."

He looked and noticed carved writing that read, "Cast all your anxiety on Him because He cares for you."[1]

---

1 1 Peter 5:7 NIV

His immediate reaction was sarcasm. He knew where that was from. Well, he knew it was somewhere in The Book, and that people used those words as a common bit of advice for the stressed-out Seeker. But soon, his sarcasm began to dissolve into a longing for the ability to cast all his anxiety away from himself. Who took it, he didn't care, but to be able to cast it off would be so greatly welcomed; it was so heavy.

His thoughts suddenly shifted back to his surroundings. *What is this place?* Obviously, someone had been here before, so keeping this place a secret was out of the question. He figured he would embrace the present and try to take it all in and capture a mental picture of the whole thing. He wanted to remember the sights and sounds and his feelings, so that he could go back here, at least in his mind, when he needed to get away from things. He sat and absorbed it all.

Because of how he had been feeling lately, being in this place at this time was so refreshing that he never wanted it to end. The pressure of feeling inadequate and never being able to do enough, to be good enough, had built up so much that he had felt ready to explode, and now it was as if someone had relieved him of this pressure, and he felt weightless and carefree. This is what he had been longing for, and he never wanted it to end. As seemingly successful as Buddy may have been, he was plagued with the constant feeling that there was something more. This persistent pressure that he felt was imposed *on* him, but also *by* him. Whenever he felt like he had reached some pinnacle or had a breakthrough, he quickly reverted to the feeling that there was something more, or that he was missing out on something else. That feeling birthed a pressure to do more, be more—and left him continually unsatisfied.

Just then, the sound of rustling leaves snapped him out of his daze, and he was instantly annoyed as he noticed a woman walking toward him. He thought, *I mean, really, with all this forest, she has to be here, now?*

As he pretended not to notice her approaching, he tried to quickly get up to carry on with his run. He didn't want to leave, but he really didn't want a companion, either. So, he decided to cut short his excursion in paradise and make his exit.

Just as he got up, his hamstring pulled tight and cramped so much so that he couldn't move. His getaway was thwarted. "Excuse me; excuse me, sir," she chirped in a very sweet voice. So, he turned around with a fake smile and replied, "Hey."

"Do you know where my canoe is?" she asked.

"Your what?" Buddy said, annoyed.

"I'm sorry to bother you, but I was told that I could follow this path and that my canoe would be somewhere around here."

"Canoe? Um, all I see is forest, and unless the canoe has wheels or unless you have a never-ending supply of water in that bottle, you might have an issue canoeing around here. Just my opinion."

Yes, it was a little brash, but he was quite amused with himself at the wittiness of his response.

She instantly lost the sweet, naïve voice, and in an equally sarcastic tone said, "Nice. Sarcasm is the lowest form of wit."

He suddenly didn't feel so witty. As she walked away, she glanced back, slightly shaking her head as if to say, "Thanks for nothing."

Phew, at least she was gone, and he could try to limp back to his spot and try once more to relish this wonderful environment. He was almost right back into his dreamy state of mind, slowly taking in all that was around him, when he heard that voice in his head repeat what the woman had said: "Do you know where my canoe is?" It was as if she believed there were canoes around there and knew she had one waiting especially for her.

What a strange bird, he thought as he chuckled to himself, *thinking that maybe his situation wasn't so bad. I mean, after all, I could be in the woods, looking for a canoe!*

But there was something about her confidence about there being a canoe for her in the middle of the woods. Had he really passed out? Was he dreaming? It just seemed too surreal that this would have taken place in Buddy's reality. He became annoyed at the fact that he was actually spending time thinking about this instead of relishing the serenity of the forest. But there was something too odd about this whole thing.

So, he decided to get up and explore a little bit of the surroundings, to see what was around and to make sure the woman wasn't a complete lunatic.

As he walked through the woods, he noticed a little opening through a set of berried bushes that seemed to lead down a hill. The path was so wooded that with all the twists and turns, he could only see a few yards ahead. He looked around to see if there were any more stray freaks looking for canoes, but the coast was clear, and he continued on the path.

It was surely leading downhill, because he noticed he had to purposely slow his pace so he didn't break into a trot. He saw that the canoe woman was only about twenty yards ahead of him. He quickly turned around and headed back, so as not to seem like he was stalking her—but then he decided it was way too intriguing, and he continued down the path. He managed to maintain a large buffer of distance between him and the Canoe Seeker. At the very least, he figured he was doing some psychiatric hospital a favor and would track down their missing patient and have a funny story to tell.

The path became less narrow and seemed to open up little by little. Suddenly, to his disbelief, he thought he heard the sound of rushing waters. He immediately thought that he did not want to see that woman again, because where there is rushing water there could be canoes, and that could lend itself to a foot-in-mouth experience. As he continued along, he saw a larger opening that led down to The River. The River's edge was quite large, with a whole section of beach that hosted canoes of various shapes, sizes, and colors. *Oh man, he thought. This is not good.*

He ducked back behind one of the larger trees and listened as he heard a Voice—which, strangely enough, sounded familiar to him. *What is going on?* Buddy thought. He was sure this was a dream, but he figured it was quite interesting and perhaps worth playing out a little longer.

As he sat behind a tree, he heard The Voice explain to the woman some details about her canoe and the apparent journey she was excitedly embarking on. A Guide approached and took her from The Voice to The River's edge, where she got in the canoe and set off downriver.

As he sat watching, he felt a warm breeze embrace his whole being. It made his eyes feel heavy and his spirit light. He thought that maybe he was getting ready to wake up from one long, strange dream, so he let his eyes close—and had started drifting off to sleep when suddenly, he felt a tap on his shoulder.

It was The Voice, nudging him and saying, "Buddy... Buuddddyyyy... it's time to wake up."

CHAPTER 2

Decision Time

"Every time you make a choice you are turning the central part of you, the part of you that chooses, into something a little different than it was before. And taking your life as a whole, with all your innumerable choices, all your life long you are slowly turning this central thing into a heavenly creature or a hellish creature: either into a creature that is in harmony with God, and with other creatures, and with itself, or else into one that is in a state of war and hatred with God, and with its fellow creatures, and with itself. To be the one kind of creature is heaven: that is, it is joy and peace and knowledge and power. To be the other means madness, horror, idiocy, rage, impotence, and eternal loneliness. Each of us at each moment is progressing to the one state or the other."

– C. S. Lewis

Expecting to wake up in his bed, nice and cozy, feeling happy and content that at least he had gone for a run in his dream, he awoke to find that he was still sitting behind the tree, but that The Voice was waking him up.

"First, Buddy, you're not dreaming. Second, the woman who just left wanted me to tell you that she found her canoe." The Voice spoke with a hint of sarcasm. *Wow, that comment worked its way right around to bite me in the rear end!*

As Buddy looked at The River, he noticed the Canoe Seeker floating down The River in her canoe, smiling confidently and pointing to her canoe, as she looked intently at him.

"Anyway," said The Voice as He smiled softly, giving a soft chuckle as He guided Buddy to The River's edge.

The Voice knew that Buddy's head was filling with questions, and He was prepared to answer them—but first, He had a question for Buddy. "Where are you?"[2]

He could tell that Buddy was contemplating this question and was about to venture a guess, when The Voice said, "This question was asked of Adam and Eve when they ate of the forbidden fruit in the Garden of Eden." He continued, "Their whereabouts were obviously known to The Creator, but where their hearts were, that was the unknown. Their act of disobedience when they ate of the fruit was from the heart. Their hearts went from being focused on The Creator to being

2 Genesis 3:9 ESV

focused on themselves and their own selfish desires. If the heart is focused on The Creator, it will be full, and marvelous wonders can take place. But if the heart is set on selfish desires, it will not be full until it has devoured everything in its path and submitted to its own selfish ambitions. I always try to catch people before they are fully devoted to themselves, because once they are at that point, they can usually only begin turning back by extreme circumstances. So, Buddy, 'Where are you?'"

The Voice paused for Buddy to contemplate the question once more, but in a deeper fashion.

Buddy suddenly felt sorry for the selfish attitudes he had been driven by these past few years. He didn't even make a mental decision to feel remorseful, but it was as if his heart was warming to the words of The Voice. His mind began to race through situations and relationships that had been damaged by the selfish leading of his heart. He began to feel nauseous and weak in the knees, because he was beginning to realize that the source of most of his dilemmas was his own selfish desires and actions.

He looked warmly at Buddy and said, "Go with it, Buddy; let your remorse go from a feeling to fruition. I hope you decide that you will let go of the selfish ambitions and desires, and let Me fill your heart with My desires and never-ending love and acceptance. Let go of what can only kill you and leave you empty, then replace it with The Gift that makes you complete. It starts with a choice, and unless you make that choice, this River is not for you." Buddy didn't know what to say. He knew that his heart was aching and longing for what The Voice was speaking about. But he also knew that the decision could cost him all the dreams and desires he was pursuing.

The Voice, recognizing that Buddy was having an internal struggle but excited that Buddy was able to correctly count the cost of this decision, began to tell him a story.

"Buddy," The Voice began, "there was once a man who was, well let's say, religious. He was diligent in doing all the things that were of a religious nature. He prayed all the time and studied to increase his knowledge beyond that of all his peers, a seemingly great example for all who looked up to him. Yet this man was doing what he thought to be right and morally correct, with little or no heed to what The Creator desired for his life specifically. I was forced to bring him to a point of recognizing Me and My vision for his life and his true call from The Creator.

"I made direct contact with him and gave him the choice to change his ways and follow Me from his heart. He made this decision because he knew that I had all the answers, and that only I had the true destiny that would make him complete and free. He knew that I held eternal life, a destiny that was offered and accepted. He also knew that I had a specific plan for his life here on this earth. Once he believed that, his heart was only content with following My plan.

"You see, he saw that I knew his true purpose, his destiny. Buddy, can you imagine if you knew that you were on the road to your personal destiny and plan for your life here on earth? Can you imagine this? Living in the understanding that you are walking step by step in the plan I have laid out for you?

"This is what I am offering you. You have accepted The Sacrifice, and you are accepted into My family; no one can take that away from you. But the decision you have before you is whether or not you want to live in fulfillment, joy, and wonder. Whether you want to exchange clichés and theories for truth and destiny. I am willing to take you down The River of Life; My River for you. If you take on this challenge, I will teach you about life, and I will personally guide you through The River, equipping you with every tool you'll ever need."

The Voice continued, "This man that I spoke of was the apostle Paul. He was not a bad man but was ruled by law and selfish ambitions. When he decided to change his heart, I entered in and reigned there. His path was straight and laid out perfectly before him. It was not all peaches and cream, yet it was *his* path; it was *his* destiny. Paul was willing to die for that destiny and for the One who filled his heart—Me.

"Buddy, would you die for the things that fill your heart now? Or would you trade frustration for glory and uncertainty for assurance? This is the choice before you. When Paul began his journey with Me, he was steadfast and diligent to serve Me and My plan. Through him, I spread My amazing Good News from one place to the ends of the known earth. Buddy, does that sound like your current path? Does that compare to the goals and dreams you have for yourself now? I am delighted that you are here before Me and that your heart is heavy. I know that your heaviness means you are finding great wisdom in what I am telling you. Your heartstrings are being pulled tight. What do you say, Buddy?"

Buddy was speechless, with so many thoughts racing through his mind. Was he happy? Was he content with his plans for his life? Would he die for the plans he had made for himself? Was his heart full, or rarely satisfied? The thought of having his heart satisfied and continually filled—was that even possible? Would he believe it? *Could* he believe it? As Buddy was gazing into The River, The Voice asked one last question, "Buddy, do you trust Me?"

All of a sudden, Buddy knew the answer. Just as he was about to respond, The Voice asked him to sit down and consider it all for a moment longer. Right then, someone came barreling down the narrow path to The River's edge.

His name was Excited, and he was young and apparently overwrought about something. He raced down the narrow path, running eagerly toward The Voice. It was as if he had run all the way from his home—as if he knew The River and The Voice—and he didn't need the extra questions or stories from The Voice, and it was to ride this River that he came.

Buddy did not hear all that transpired between The Voice and Excited, but he saw that there was an immediate trust and excitement on Excited's part toward both The Voice and The River. Excited ran over and expectantly investigated several dozen canoes and then, as if he had just won some lottery that only he knew about, he looked at The Voice and smiled. A more thankful and genuine smile Buddy had never seen. It was as if someone had just opened the perfect present on Christmas morning. A present that he had only known in his heart, and yet someone had picked out that exact gift.

As Excited picked up his canoe and walked it to The River's edge, he noticed that his name was carved on the front and back of the canoe. It was his canoe, and it looked different from all the others. In fact, as Buddy inspected the canoes more closely, he noticed that none of the canoes were the same, and they were all personally inscribed with a different name. Even the way the name was engraved on the canoes was distinct and unique.

Just then, he looked over and saw Excited being pushed out into the middle of The River, looking happier than Buddy had ever seen anyone. As Buddy watched Excited float down The River, he noticed The Voice walking back over toward him, smiling as He walked.

"So, what's your answer, Buddy? Where are you?" said The Voice.

"I think I'm ready," Buddy said with a childish excitement. "I'm in, but what was the deal with Excited? I mean, it was as if this was a given for him—as if he knew this was for him, and he was expecting that you would have a canoe just for him. How did he know that? And why was he so excited?"

The Voice responded, "Excited was just forgiven much. His excitement is because his decision to accept The Gift is fresh, and he has just been brought to the place of refreshing and triumph over sin and emptiness. Excited was also discipled by a true believer. The believer who discipled him taught him many truths of the life which is now before him, and what to expect, as well as how to handle the unexpected. The believer told Excited about The River, and that The River provided a time of intimate discipleship, laying the foundations for a life with The Voice and The Guide; that it was necessary to travel down The River and be mentored by them. He was also taught that life wasn't stress-free and wouldn't all be easily swallowed, but that there was great joy and fulfillment ahead. Excited was eager, because he knew that The River was a way to know God and to grasp hold of his personal plan, equipping him to be able to recognize the steps set before him. He knew that The River was a vital part of his new life and Decision."

"I can vaguely recall that feeling," remarked Buddy. "And funnily enough, I feel that being stirred up again inside my heart."

"Make no mistake, Buddy, you did not happen upon this River. I knew you were ready and I made your path lead here. I used your desire for a challenge, your desire for peace, and your curiosity to lead you right here, right now," said The Voice.

Buddy was beginning to feel an excitement grow within him about the upcoming journey and the chance to know The Creator, The Voice, and whoever else would come along. He was desperate to see where he was meant to be and what he was created for. *Imagine,* he thought, *if I knew exactly why I was created and I was able to walk in that perfect plan—now that's cool.*

The Voice could anticipate that Buddy was getting a little ahead of himself, so He relayed a brutal truth to him. "Unfortunately, many people's excitement for the perfect path ends with excitement. The first sign of trouble or the stripping off of the first layer oftentimes gives Seekers a sour taste and tempts them to abandon the path and the lessons it affords. They think they can just keep Me in their pocket for a rainy day, thinking that the fullness of this process is optional."

The Voice continued, "Buddy, you could not imagine the number of people I bring down to The River's edge to begin their journey, but they get fearful and leave, never getting to know Me or grasping their destiny with Me."

"Fearful of what?" Buddy asked.

"Fearful of change. Many people desire change, but My change comes with a price. Just as you, before our meeting here at The River's edge, made a Decision to follow Me, but all you did was incorporate a few beliefs into your existing life. You never gave over 100 percent of yourself to Me. You basically continued on your prior path and used Me as a good luck charm. I'm not a good luck charm, Buddy. I am not a trinket that you wear around your neck, or something you hang on your wall. I would rather you leave now and live your life on your own than treat Me like a trinket. I need all of you, not a piece. If a piece is all you can give Me, I will reject it. Sadly, when many people find out this truth, they leave. They count the cost and decide that their life without Me is better than the prospect of a new one with Me.

They know that they will have to change, and they're scared.

"Buddy, I have more respect when people walk away and decide they do not want change than when people try to use Me as a good luck charm or a spice to add to their existing path. I am none of those things. You, Buddy, have contemplated the options and the costs and have decided that I am worth it."

CHAPTER 3

The Stripping Process

"Lift up thyn heart unto God, with a meek stirring of love and mean (long for) himself and none of his goods."
– Unknown Author, *The Cloud of Unknowing*

"What you just told me about 'stripping off the first layer'—well, what gets stripped, and how?" Buddy questioned hesitantly.

"Yes, the stripping process is something we need to talk about," explained The Voice.

"You see, you've accumulated many things that are not part of My perfect plan: physical, spiritual, and mental things. I need to remove those from you to make sure that you are equipped for *your* path. Some of these hindrances you can lay down on the beach before we get you into your canoe. Others are more ingrained and have attached themselves to your innermost being. Therefore, they will require some more abrasive circumstances to remove them. These hindrances that have attached themselves can be so hidden that you don't even know they are there, yet they are the catalysts that result in many poor decisions and self-serving and self-defensive tendencies. We need to have a total removal of these items.

"This is a process, and often the importance of it is overlooked. There is a parable about putting new wine into old wineskins. I am not sure if you are familiar with it, but do you know why this would be a bad idea?" asked The Voice.

"Um, well, I guess that the old wineskins might not be strong enough to hold the new wine?" Buddy said reluctantly, actually beginning to realize that this River, although exciting, might get uncomfortable.

"Correct," The Voice replied. "It is the same concept here. I am about to pour into you living water, life, vision, and purpose that are not consistent with your old ways. Many believe that this process is a magical one, where one day you are a sinner and then you make a decision and poof, you're a saint. There is some truth to that; however, to live and to love like a saint, you must relinquish the old ways and exchange them for ways that will work together with sainthood. You need an overhaul, Buddy. Does this concept sound familiar?" The Voice questioned.

"Kind of," replied Buddy.

"Buddy, what could the difficulty be with this instant magical change theory?" The Voice inquired.

"Well, I suppose if you believe you are magically changed, there wouldn't be much motivation or even need to go down The River," Buddy answered sheepishly.

"Right, my friend, and that's where we have our problem. I try to take people down The River to extract and discipline those hindrances out of them, and they begin to think that they are being punished. If you live in a materialistic society, you will be more accustomed to luxury, excess, and prosperity. Sometimes those things make their way into the theories of My Seekers. Don't make the mistake of thinking that the only things I desire for you are riches and safety. I do want you to have your needs provided for. There is no blanket statement for the amount of money I want you to have or the number of things that I permit you to amass. However, if you have a lot, I have one question for you: Are you living in luxury while your neighbor is unsure of where his next meal will come from? And by your neighbor, I mean anyone you encounter."

The Voice continued, "Seekers living in places of wealth often think that I have put them there to enjoy the finer things, that it is solely a reward for good behavior. When in fact, I have put them there to try to bring a balance to overindulgence, modesty to daily living, and an ability to benefit those in need. When they ignore that, they ignore Me and My plan for them. Soon enough, they forget about Me and only remember their things. One of My most disheartening experiences is bringing someone to a place of wealth, getting them into all the right situations and opportunities, and elevating them up so that they can provide for others and for My causes. Then they become comfortable with luxuries and forget the purpose of their good fortune.

"Buddy, I prepare Seekers for situations that they will soon encounter. For instance, since we are on the topic of money, I know that someone will come into a surplus of money, and I know the exact hour it'll happen. So, I bring upon them situations that will prepare them and provoke them to build a foundation of modesty and self-control. If someone heeds those lessons, they will be well prepared for the money and how to use it, whether they spend it or use it to provide for My purposes. If they ignore Me and bypass My lessons leading up to the event, they will not be prepared and will therefore not walk out My perfect plan for them and the provision.

"I also create beautiful opportunities where those in need come together with those with much. I bring the prospect of a magnificent story of true love, sharing, and sacrifice for others. But then, those with much turn selfish and hoard with a closed fist the gifts they have so freely received. This happens often. I know what will happen to you and when it will happen. I will always bring situations that will teach you lessons and prepare you for upcoming circumstances, both good and bad ones. I will bring you many opportunities to show kindness, love, and compassion. It's up to you to see these opportunities through and to not get caught up in yourself. Buddy, you must listen to Me, seek Me, and I will allow Myself and My lessons to be found by you.[3]

"Never be complacent in anything. Complacency is the easiest and most common tactic of The Destroyer. He uses it to make you lazy and distracted, and to rob you of the fighting spirit inside of you. Keep fighting, Buddy, for I have given you a purpose which only you can accomplish in the way I desire it done. So, go forth and conquer, following My lead at every step!" The Voice exclaimed with passion.

"Destroyer?" Buddy questioned. "That doesn't sound good."

"It's not good, Buddy, but I will talk about him later. For now, just know that he only has as much power as you give him—nothing more and nothing less. First, some more important questions for you," The Voice said, while motioning for Buddy to sit in the sand.

"Buddy, do you know your biggest need?" The Voice asked.

---

3 1 Chronicles 28:9 (author paraphrase)

"Um, food?" he muttered with uncertainty.

"Food is important, but what kind of food?" asked The Voice.

"Vegetables?" Buddy replied, fairly confident that he had gotten that one right. The Voice let out a friendly chuckle and put His hand on Buddy's shoulder. Leaning into him, He said, "No Buddy, the most important food is the food I give you—the food that nourishes the soul. My words to you are nourishment enough to sustain you through any crisis, as well as times of joy. You need to eat every day in order to sustain your physical body, right?"

"Yeah," Buddy responded.

"Okay, so in the same way that you need physical food every day, you also need to listen to My words for you every day. Bottom line, Buddy, don't forget about Me, and never put our relationship on cruise control. Do you know what the default setting is on your ability to relate with Me?" asked The Voice.

"Overdrive," Buddy said, wanting to sound zealous.

"Well, no; actually, your default setting is complacency. You see, I teach those I love. and I discipline them to help them grow. If you are on this River, you know that I love you. You must keep in mind that I am with you at every step. You may not always see Me or hear My voice, but I am there, because My words and presence are always around you. I know this River, and more importantly, I know you and what you need to learn and discover on this River.

"So, always pay attention to Me first, and always listen and keep in your heart the words I give to you. This River can be fierce at times, and it will cause you pain when you begin. But the better you understand the process and the lessons to be learned, and you hold on to the fact that you are being refined, the more you will receive, and the better your attitude and reliance upon Me will be. This will make for a bright future of obedience that blossoms into true friendship.

"This process," The Voice began to explain, "is about breaking up the fallow ground. There is a story in The Book about a guy named Hosea. It is a story about a prophet whom The Creator called to marry an unfaithful woman. The story is about sorrow, shame, and love. There is an adulterous woman who is never faithful to her husband, yet the husband still yearns for her, still seeks her, and tries to restore their relationship. There is a verse in that book that says, 'Sow with a view to righteousness, reap in accordance with kindness; break up your fallow ground, for it is time to seek the Lord until He comes to rain righteousness on you.'[4]

"This River will be hard at times and refreshing at times, but remember this—I will never leave you. Even when you prostitute yourself to other things, I will seek

4 Hosea 10:12 NASB

you out with an undying love. Breaking up your fallow ground means making sure that you are open to My instruction and discipline, getting rid of the things that separate us like greed, selfishness, hate, and complacency. Fallow ground is uncultivated ground; it has no moisture and is hard as rock; nothing can grow there. Once the ground begins to be broken up and cultivated, it can become rich soil that grows magnificent crops. That is Me raining righteousness upon you. The raining of righteousness is My job. Your job is to allow your field to be cultivated and your heart to be softened. Don't stop seeking Me and cultivating the depths of your fallow heart until I produce great, everlasting riches in it.

"Buddy, the works of My hands, My people, are continuously adulterous in their relationship toward Me. They seek other things and forget about Me all the time. This River experience is about a lifestyle—a lifestyle that says, 'I will seek the Lord and find peace and fulfillment in Him and the things He wants to show me.' Buddy, I am telling you all of this because it is time for you to 'break up your fallow ground.' That means to take what you have sown in selfishness, reaping rewards of selfish indulgence, and instead, sow with righteousness. What you will reap is Me, raining My gifts of love, encouragement, fulfillment, and peace into your life.

"I will grant to you gifts and situations that are in line with My righteousness, things that perfectly align with My plan for you. And that plan is marvelous. Breaking up fallow ground will hurt—it must hurt. To get through to the good soil, we must break through all those bad thoughts and actions. We must rip out unbelief and faithlessness by the roots. However, don't despair, Buddy, because this process will bring about rich, new soil that will reap My perfect harvest.

"Will you allow Me to break up your fallow ground, Buddy?" The Voice asked politely.

Buddy understood that this would probably cause a lot of pain and discomfort, but it was as if something dead inside of him was coming to life. As if he suddenly realized that what he thought would come about by the magical waving of a wand, he now understood would require a process to transform from death to life and to turn from being miserable to being fulfilled. It was this process he wanted to say yes to, despite the treacherous waters that might lead him there.

The Voice went on to explain to Buddy a parable and picture that better described the process as a whole. "Buddy, do you remember the story of the sower[5] scattering seeds, and the seeds falling on different types of soil?"

"Yes, I believe so," Buddy said. "What I remember is that the seeds grew in the good soil," he said, very pleased with himself that he knew the answer.

---

5 Matthew 13:1-23

"You're right, Buddy," The Voice said approvingly. "The seed did indeed thrive in the good soil. But Buddy, this parable is about the whole process I need you to go through. And this process does not end until you are with Me beyond the Waterfall. You will get better at it in time, but My hope is that you will engage this River your whole life and continue learning, growing, and living a fulfilled life—your life as it was meant to be.

"Buddy, the first part of this process requires faith and surrender. You must surrender your rights. Lay down what is perishable in exchange for what is imperishable and never trade back, no matter how attractive and alluring it may be. Surrender is the hardest part of the process. You are forgoing your desires, dreams, and ambitions, exchanging your rags for My riches. As far as the parable goes, you must surrender the field first, which is your life. Surrender your life to Me so that I can cultivate and break up your fallow ground.

"You are going to be amazed at what you get in return for what you give up. Most people never surrender their field to Me, because they don't think that My plan could be better than theirs and they don't want to give up control of their lives. Consider that you are not giving up control to One who is far from you and is ignorant of your potential. Remember that you are surrendering to the One who spoke all of creation into being and is in control of everything. I am the One who creates and sustains all beauty and fulfillment. Surrender to Me, Buddy, and you will abide in My abundance.

"The Sower sowed the same seed on a few different types of soil. And as you so rightly answered, the seed grew in the rich soil; I am that Sower. I need you to see that I know what is best for you, and it is in your best interest to let Me cultivate your soil and produce the perfect crop for your life. Sometimes I start this process and you can be 100 percent on board. However, when The River turns harsh and you are tired and discouraged, you will be tempted to quit. Some will try to convince you that I don't exist, and others will attempt to debate you about the validity of My instructions to you. The farther you allow yourself to stray from your time alone with Me, the easier it will be for you to listen to their empty theories.

"Regardless of what people tell you, or what others try to deceive you with during this time, I will always be with you—never forget! You will also face the temptation to settle for what I've done already in the past and cease anticipating what is to come. Just as I know the right ways for you to travel down The River, I also know the full measure of time that you need to develop in each series of events. Have you ever tried to eat something that needs to be baked for one hour, and you try to eat it after it's only been in the oven for fifteen minutes? It's not done; there has not been enough time to allow the food to form the proper consistency and taste.

"There are designated times for each of your trials and tests. Don't ever settle for second best or worldly wisdom, Buddy. It will leave you unsatisfied and settling for what seems good rather than what is best. When the time is more appropriate, I will share with you the lessons of some people who have gone before you down this River.

"Getting back to the story of the soil and the seed, I can make the soil perfect, but if you don't let Me finish the process, weeds, thorns, and other deterrents can grow *at any point*. So, I may begin a work in you and commence with a portion of the field—your field. Then, as I get a portion ready, you may see that I have done a great work in that portion, and you may be tempted to think that enough work has been done. After all, this portion is better than you could have ever imagined it could be. You may not see the need for the whole field to be made ready.

"Don't back out early, Buddy. Make sure that I get to complete the process and prepare the whole field for My seed. Until I can cultivate and make ready the entire field, you will not be living your destiny. Don't let thorns and weeds grow up; keep My lessons in your heart, and let your faith grow into a beautiful crop. The crop that I desire for everyone is great faith. Many Seekers think that I want tremendous sacrifices, or extreme giving, or hours upon hours of prayer, but these things are an outflow of great faith. The more you believe (have faith) in Me and My capabilities, the greater you will be, and the more meaningful and complete your life will be."

Without feeling anything, or maybe he was feeling everything, Buddy began to cry. Tears rolled down his face because things began to make sense. He knew there was truth—answers to so many of the *whys* in life—but being taught firsthand here on The River was an overwhelming moment that Buddy didn't fully know how to handle.

The Voice, sensing that Buddy's innermost being was absorbing all He was saying, continued with a knowing smile, "I have given you The Book to meditate with, study, and memorize. This will be like living water to your soul when you are thirsty. Never stop engaging with what's in The Book, because your faith will be compounded just by dwelling on its truth. Without faith, it is impossible to please Me.[6]

"Remember to keep it simple, Buddy, and allow your faith to grow in the face of every kind of situation. Great faith, Buddy—great faith!"

---

6 Hebrews 11:6 ESV

CHAPTER 4

The Reason for the River

"It is one thing to believe in God;
it is quite another to believe God."
– R. C. Sproul

Buddy's emotions roiled within him. His tears had lessened, but the new understanding he had grasped was still overwhelming. The Voice identified his feelings and continued. "You will be tempted to finish in the flesh what was begun in the spirit. Meaning that you will at first heed My direction and then try to figure out the rest on your own, in your own wisdom, rather than in My wisdom and in My time. I have this challenge with Seekers quite often. They listen to Me and hear Me in the beginning but then lose the patience that is required to build faith.

"Buddy, did you hear Me?" The Voice asked intently.

"I think so," Buddy replied. "I think I understand."

"I know that you heard Me, and that you believe you understand, but soon you will have the chance to have it abide in your heart and allow it to impact your life," The Voice said.

"So, Buddy, do you know what I desire from My Seekers most of all?"

"Their love?" asked Buddy.

"Yes, I do, but more so, their faith. It may seem simplistic, but faith is what binds us together. Faith is the adhesive that connects us. The greater faith you have in Me, the greater your love for Me, and the stronger and more resilient our relationship is. Faith is what I desire from you. Faith is what I have desired from the beginning.

"Many people think I desire sacrifices and giving things up, but I just want them to believe in Me and in My purposes for them—to trust and obey, ever increasing in faith. You have no idea, Buddy, where I can take you in this life, if your desire and effort go wholeheartedly into seeking to build your faith in Me. Once you are on that road, you will know Me and you will love Me, as you see the endlessness of My love and devotion toward you. You will then have no other response than to fall in love with Me. Let Me take you back in time for a bit of a history lesson.

"Along your journey on The River, like I said before, I will show you in detail some stories about certain Seekers who have gone before you. These stories will allow you to see My plan—the big picture on which to build your foundation. But right now, I want to get you started with the story of a very special Seeker—you've most likely heard of him. This is the story of a boy who surrendered to Me, and in turn was humbled and then exalted in a greater way than he could have ever imagined.

"This Seeker was faithful to Me. The only complaint anyone could have about this young man was that he may have been a little naïve. It turns out that because of household jealousy, he was ripped from his family—losing his comforts and all he knew—to be dragged to a foreign country as a slave. This young man was put into forced labor at a very young age. Okay, maybe he was a tad selfish and naïve, as many young people are, but did he deserve to be ripped from his family and sent to a foreign land to do a slave's work?

"He continually tried to make the best of the situation, and he remained faithful to Me. He faced a trial with his boss's wife, but he continuously acted with integrity. Still, he was wrongfully accused and thrown into prison, where he remained faithful to Me and to those he was required to submit to. This young man was continually loyal to Me and to his bosses, and he was respectful to all people, even though he was mistreated at every turn.

"During all this time, I was there, leading his steps and guiding his path. Buddy, do you think when I was leading him into slavery and when he was put into prison that he thought I would cause him to become the second greatest man in the known world? Probably not, right? Right. The tendency would be to get mad at Me and even to curse Me for not looking out for him or keeping him comfortable. He didn't get bitter because his family was getting away with something that was so wrong and hurtful. He resisted those reactions and stayed faithful to Me.

"While he was in prison, he was given the opportunity to interpret dreams for very important men who 'knew all the right people.' Because he relied on Me and knew that I was in control and could interpret the dreams, he gave the interpretation of those dreams. After he interpreted the dream with a favorable outcome for one of the men, he turned to him and said, 'Only keep me in mind when it goes well with you, and please do me a kindness by mentioning me to the Pharaoh and get me out of this house.'[7]

"So Joseph, as you can see this story is about, as patient as he was, sought his own way out of his situation in prison. I put Joseph in that situation, knowing he was unable to leave even if he wanted to. That's also a position I put many of My Seekers into, so that they

7 Genesis 40:14 NASB

cannot escape easily from the important lessons I want to teach them. But Joseph was looking for an early escape, which by all rights he would have deserved, except for the fact that I was not quite ready to bring about the fullness of My plan for him.

"Buddy, imagine if I had released Joseph from prison when he asked. Could he have ever imagined the glorious position I was about to put him in? No. Let's look at the likely story that would have unfolded had Joseph been given his wish to leave prison at that time.

"More than likely, he would have traveled to his home to be reunited with his family, thinking he was free and finally in My will again. He would have been content dwelling there in the safety of his home and family. The Egyptians would have starved in the famine, not to mention how the famine would have impacted him and his family in a few years.

"Can you believe how much his ability to stick out his current circumstances changed history? If Joseph had gotten his way, he would have settled for a trip home to his family rather than My great fortune and fulfillment. Do you think he would have traded one for the other if he knew both options were on the table? Don't ever trade what looks good for what's best."

The Voice continued, "Faith is the key to your successful and intimate walk with Me throughout your journey here. Faith in Me is what lights your path and gives you peace in times of trouble—and My strength in times of your weakness. I will start you off with some small obstacles so you can practice having faith in Me, and then when the larger trials take place, you will be equipped with everything you need to pass through the testing waters and grow closer to Me and My perfect work that I promised to complete in you.

"Your act of trusting and having faith in Me is like a child who is helped across a puddle by his parent. Imagine the child needing to leap over some small puddles to get where he's going. To avoid getting wet, he must leap at the right time and exert himself to jump over the puddle, thus accomplishing the task.

"But when he encounters a larger puddle and must learn to leap over it, he relies on the strength of the parent, who is holding his hand, to help thrust him over.

"For smaller puddles, the help of the parent may seem unnecessary. But the small ones are only practice in trusting the strength of One greater for when the larger puddles come. The child must know that the adult will help him or her over a puddle of any size, but it is important that the child get into the habit and comfort of trusting in the strength and wisdom of the adult.

"Soon the child will face a puddle that is impossible to leap over on his own. He must remember all those little puddles (tests of faith) that have gone successfully and leap at the beginning of the puddle, and then trust in the adult to take him the rest of the way. The puddles will successively grow in size and complexity, but the practice will be the same: trust in the adult and rely on their strength. Buddy, I am that adult, and for as long as you are on this earth seeking My ways, you are that child."

For the first time, Buddy began to understand the nature of the relationship The Voice had been calling him to. Not to mention how that "magical transformation," where everything in life suddenly becomes perfect, was a complete load of rubbish. He was on the cusp of grasping this whole process—in theory. Suddenly, he realized that the purpose of The River was to transform all this theory into practice, to penetrate the heart and not just the head. He suddenly became curious as to how his walk would have been different if he had found out about or been open to this process earlier.

The Voice, understanding his internal dialogue, suggested, "You were not ready before, and had not recognized or experienced those situations I needed you to experience until now. But now, Buddy, you are ready, and if you so choose, you can embark on this transformational journey that is not magical, but miraculous, and is not attained overnight, but is everlasting."

He marveled, realizing that The Voice had him here at the perfect time, and that The Voice's excited willingness to invest in Buddy was a little overwhelming.

The Voice was so interested in Buddy, and he had never experienced that wholehearted devotion from anyone else, ever. It caused him to feel an instant connection and attraction to The Voice. It was just like the ambiance of his surroundings that he had felt while he was sitting on the log in the woods, soaking up his environment. He wanted to soak up this feeling and keep it with him.

"Buddy, make sure you keep that feeling with you and hold it in your heart, because there will be times in the coming days when you will be told differently, and you will feel and think differently from the way you do right now. You will be challenged to disregard Me and the things that I have told you; to follow your own wisdom and to rely on yourself. But remember how you feel about Me now, and remember that the child could have never jumped over those larger puddles without help from the adult and by relying upon that strength. Buddy, never doubt in the night what you heard in the day. Never second guess what you know I've told you when times, circumstances, or relationships become difficult. The Guide will remind you of the things I have told you in the light."

He handed Buddy The Book. "You must also read from this Book daily to remember, build, and increase your faith in Me. Start by reading a portion in the morning to set the tone for the day. Beginning your day with this will allow you to become focused and prepared for the day ahead. What if a businessman goes to work in sweatpants? Is he dressed for the job? What if a doctor goes to work in shorts and a tank top? Would he be dressed for the occasion?

"In the same way, prepare yourself, and dress your heart and mind accordingly. Be prepared to face trials every day—and that way, you won't be surprised or upset when what you don't expect to happen, happens. Likewise, finish your day by reading some of the things written in this Book, so you will be able to close your day by remembering My promises for you and reflecting on what I have done for you that day.

"I have given these things to you so that you may have success in everything I put before you. Every day that it is not read and used to build your faith, Buddy, you are one step closer to failing. Also, as often as you can, pick two separate times during the day. During the first allotted time, think of My character—all the things I have done and said. Remember who I am. This will remind you that all things are possible, every day. In the second allotted time, just dwell in nature and realize that I've created everything you see. Remember My ability and creativity. Let them inspire you and remind you of who you are connected to.

"If you cease reading and thinking of Me, you will stop remembering all My plans and being attentive to My provisions when they come. That, in turn, will make you weak and unsatisfied, and you already know what it feels like to live like that. Don't ever go back there, Buddy. You're better than that, and I believe in you."

CHAPTER 5

What to Expect

"Calm seas never made skilled sailors."
– Old English proverb

As Buddy began letting his mind run wild and his heart fill with excitement from the words and intimacy of The Voice, he grew eager to get on The River. In the midst of Buddy's excitement, The Voice spoke.

"Buddy, there is an old English saying: 'Calm seas never made skilled sailors,' and this is the same with your walk with Me. If it were all calm seas and carefree living, as you first thought it was, what would you learn? The things you would learn would be from selfish ambition, not selfless transformation. This River is fraught with deceivers and those who do not want you to succeed. They will, at all costs, attempt to redirect you and discourage you in your journey.

"But if you have faith *in Me* and accept the challenge to work through situations and circumstances that will increase your faith, you will succeed. Will you experience failure? Probably. As with any other lessons, you may not succeed on the first try, but if you continue walking toward Me and the things I have told you, you will be refined and will come one step closer to My perfect will for you.

"Buddy, remember that I know what you need, and I will direct you to the perfect place of peace, so trust Me and believe. You will get hurt, Buddy. We spoke about how the breaking up of fallow ground is not always pleasant, but as My Seeker Job dictated to his friends, 'Behold, how happy is the man whom God reproves, so do not despise the discipline of the Almighty. For He inflicts pain, and gives relief; He wounds, and His hands also heal.'[8]

"I am the one who can hurt and heal. Nobody else can deliver both, but many can and will hurt you. It may feel like they are giving you some discipline and teaching you a lesson, but they will not have the capacity to heal you and allow you to grow from the hurt. You are in faithful hands when you are with Me, Buddy.

"Some Seekers begin to think that they are just being punished while I am actually discipling them. There is a stark difference between being discipled and being punished. Discipline is My instrument to bring about solid and consistent growth in you; it allows Me to make you more like the person you are meant to be. I

---

8 Job 5:17-18 NASB

disciple and discipline those whom I love,[9] and I teach them My ways so that they will be able to overcome and succeed where they have only had heartache and failures in the past.

"Welcome this process, Buddy, and you will be welcoming a walk of freedom and truth with Me. You will not only know about Me and My character, but you will also know Me as a Friend and a perfect Father—a Father who always loves, always watches, and always has your true destiny at heart."

The Voice asked, "Do you believe that I know what is best for you on this River?"

Buddy nodded in agreement.

"Well, then, trust Me that I know what is best for you and what your perfect plan looks like. I know every step before you take it, and I will allow you to be guided down the true path. That being said, don't ever desire someone else's canoe, tools, or path down The River."

The Voice said sternly, "Someone else's path, or even their canoe, may look so much more appealing than yours, but know this: I have made your path and your canoe, as well as the tools I have given you, to be adequate for your specific journey. As appealing as someone else's 'things' may seem, they are not for you. If you start seeking what others have, you will become dissatisfied with what I have given you—and once you ingest

---

9 Hebrews 12:6-11, Proverbs 3:11-12, 1 Corinthians 11:32

even a little of that toxin, it will poison you every time. Desire what I have given you, Buddy, and nothing else.

"You must differentiate between what seems good and what My will is for you. Many words of wisdom will seem—well, like wise words. But that does not mean they are My words. You must seek My will, and there you will find peace and completeness. Many will offer you advice, and I want you to consider that I may use other Seekers to reveal parts of My will to you. However, you must learn to differentiate between the two: earthly wisdom and My wisdom. You will understand what I am speaking of very shortly.

"Lastly, Buddy, you must fight. There are those who do not want you to succeed. Some will make that known with great clarity, while others will be more deceptive in their plots to dissuade you from the path of truth. Keep your eyes open and your ears alert to The Deceiver and those who walk in his ways. Remember that you are fighting to know Me, so settle for nothing less. Many will not want you to reach that end. You are in a fight, and the only one who can authorize defeat is you; no one can take anything away from you except that which you offer them. Keep guard and follow Me."

Buddy began following The Voice up a small cliff overlooking some rapids downriver. Once they reached the top, as The Voice gazed further down The River, Buddy suddenly became overwhelmed with fear of the reality of what was ahead of him. For the first time, he saw a glimpse of what The Voice had been speaking about all this time.

The rapids looked fierce. Thoughts began to swirl around in his head. What did he know about The River, or about canoes and surviving those ferocious waters? *I'm going to die*, he thought, as he began to be filled with doubts and fears. Could he maneuver through such unknown territory? *After all*, he thought, *this is all so new to me, and can I really be expected to conquer such a task as this?* He soon felt dumbstruck with feelings of inadequacy, lack of training, and unfamiliarity with what was to come, but right then The Voice nudged him and said, "Easy now, Buddy; you're going to have to get that under control. Fear and doubt will kill almost any dream and will most definitely decelerate—if not derail—your successful walk with Me.

"Take control, Buddy, and remember that when you became My friend, you surrendered all of that rubbish too. Your fear and doubt are mine now. I take them from you and they disappear within Me, because fear and doubt cannot live within perfect love and the confidence that follows. Yes, you will take them back from time to time, but remember that at any time I will collect them back and take care of them for you. All you must do is to cast your burdens on Me and know that I will incinerate them for you. Do you remember your efforts to try to walk this walk on your own strength? Yes? I do too, and they didn't amount to much, other than frustration and compromise. When you feel like you don't need Me or My Guide, remember the frustrations of your own efforts and rely on Me.

"Buddy, you will soon learn that My ways and My thoughts are so full and deep that you could not even begin to imagine the wonderful plans I have for you[10] on this River and the places beyond. Simply trust Me and ride down this River with Me. Rely on The Guide, and resist The Deceiver and all of those who follow him. Then you will succeed in finding peace and My perfect plan for you."

The Voice said this with such conviction and confidence—but also with so much love and compassion—that Buddy felt no other response but to take hold of that fear and doubt and cast it to The Voice. He actually made a physical motion, as if to dig out those thoughts of fear and doubt and throw them upon the shoulders of The Voice. It seemed silly, but he felt a release and a glimmer of hope that he could do this if he would rely on his Friend.

"One final thing before you set foot in your canoe. I want you to take some time under that willow tree down by The River's edge and write. Write down how you feel right now and about this whole process. Write

10 Isaiah 55:8-9, Isaiah 40:28-31, Psalm 139:1-6, Romans 11:33-34

everything you are feeling about this upcoming journey and about your past failures. Write about your journey up to this point, and whether it has left you feeling satisfied or unsatisfied.

"Buddy, be real, and get it out and begin to process the enormity of your upcoming journey. You are about to go from being uninformed and naïve to becoming faithful and informed. You need to know what you're fighting for, Buddy. You need to realize that all your fear and doubt that have led you down the road of frustration are about to be uprooted. As we talked about earlier, this will cause some pain, but that pain will lead to freedom and peace. Make sure you write down and know what you are fighting for, and that the pain and sweat will be worth it."

As Buddy followed the advice of his Friend, The Voice, he knew that this was important, so he began frantically scribbling down single words that turned into pages of his thoughts and emotions that were released as if a floodgate had burst forth in his soul. He wrote about his failures, his fears, his doubts, and all of his struggles; and how he was so looking forward to finally knowing what a real walk with this Friend would be.

He soon found that his writing was getting quite sloppy because of the speed with which he was thinking and scribing. After a few hours of what seemed like five minutes, he gave a huge sigh and felt a warm breeze brush over his face. The breeze seemed magical, and whether it was the release of writing and getting all of that out or a coincidence, he knew that this was exactly where he was meant to be.

CHAPTER 6

Laying It All Down

"He is no fool who gives what he cannot keep
to gain what he cannot lose."
– Jim Elliot

Buddy walked over to his Friend, The Voice, with the pad of paper he had used to journal his thoughts and feelings, and began to put it into his backpack to save for later.

"I'll take that," his Friend said sternly.

"Oh, I thought I would save that for later," Buddy said reluctantly.

"Well, I'm going to ask you to lay down everything you have, and then I will return what you need—what I see fit for you to have on this journey," The Friend said.

"You see," The Friend continued, "along the way, as you were walking in your own strength and wisdom, you have accumulated many things that have weighed you down and others that have distracted you. I want to make sure you do not have any excess baggage and are

not without some tools you will need. So, take everything off, leave everything behind, and I will give you
new clothes, and a new bag for your journal and The
Book. The Guide has prepared everything for you, as
well as some other tools for your journey."

Buddy began to take everything off and relin-
quished whatever he had with him on The River's edge.
The Friend took the items and put them in a hole in
the ground. He then brought Buddy new, waterproof
clothing suited just for The River. Buddy thought they
looked quite comfortable and put them on. There was
also a waterproof bag with a watertight seal. The Friend
put The Book and the journal in the sack and handed it
to Buddy.

"These are to stay with you, and make sure that dust
does not collect on these. Use them as frequently as I
have instructed you."

As Buddy was taking all of this in and getting prepared for the journey ahead, he was now less worried
about the rapids and more worried that he might need
something he had been instructed to leave behind. The
Friend disappeared, and The Guide was standing in
front of him.

Buddy's experience with The Guide was strange
at first. He knew that there was a person standing in
front of him, but He never spoke audibly. It was as if
His words were spoken in the heart and head of Bud-

dy. It was a little strange at first, and Buddy had a hard time deciphering whether it was his own internal voice or if it was, in fact, The Guide speaking to his heart and mind directly.

Weird, thought Buddy; but in the same way, there was something tender and very personal about the way they communicated.

The Guide spoke through that internal small, still voice, and instructed Buddy to go where the canoes were and look for the one for him. Buddy walked over to the canoes quite excitedly, swiftly looking over all the canoes, scanning them for the one that seemed to be just for him. After all, he remembered Excited and the woman he first saw in woods, and how they had been so excited to find their own unique canoes.

As Buddy scanned a few dozen canoes he found one with his name on it, etched on the side in some of the coolest writing he had ever seen. As if someone had etched his name with fire into the side of the canoe, it was glowing and looked magnificent. The brilliance of the etching almost allowed him to ignore the fact that his canoe looked a bit more like a rowboat than a canoe. It was larger than the rest, which brought him some comfort, because it seemed like it could be fairly stable on The River. He was okay with that, because he was still quite nervous about the rapids right around the bend.

Even though he was happy that his boat was larger than the rest, he thought there was no way he could carry it down to The River's edge. As he thought about how impossible the task of just dragging it would be, he heard the voice of The Guide say in his head, "Try it; don't doubt. Just do it."

He reluctantly took his canoe from among the others, and with a loud grunt, began to drag it down to The River's edge where The Guide was waiting for him.

Although the canoe was bulkier than the rest of them, he had no problem dragging it down to The River's edge. He was a little embarrassed about the grunt he had let out when he first went to pick it up, because it actually took very little effort. In fact, he did not have to struggle at all.

As he thought this, he heard The Guide's voice in his mind say, "You will never be given a load that is too much for both you and The Friend to handle; you will always be able to bear it together. Sometimes it may look too heavy, too much of a burden—but if The Friend has placed it in your path, you will be able to bear any burden or accomplish any task with His help. Your only problem comes when you try to do too much or the wrong thing with it. Listen to My voice and know that The Friend is always there to help you. Never forget that, Buddy. You would not believe how many people see their canoes and never pick them up because they think they are too much to bear. They miss out on so much because they doubt themselves—and more so, the direction of The Friend.

"The Friend and I work in tandem. I only speak what is in line with what The Friend is instructing you to do. The more you listen for My guidance, the clearer it will be for you, and the better you will be at deciphering My voice from your own voice. I do not want you to ever doubt that you heard Me. One of the greatest lies of The Destroyer is to make Seekers believe that they did not hear Me correctly, and that it was their own voice and not Mine speaking to them. The Destroyer will use any tactic possible to try to have you fail on this River, to have you quit and settle for mediocre and nominal rather than complete fulfillment. Don't quit, don't doubt—and don't ever, ever forget that you are on this River for a reason; and even if you don't see the reasons right away, I will expose them to you at the right time. You are here for a reason, Buddy. If you follow through and don't give up, you will learn more and become more than you ever could on your own.

"Do you like flowers, Buddy? I mean, do you appreciate flowers?"

Buddy nodded affirmatively, because he really did appreciate beautiful flowers.

"Well, if that flower is given poor soil and limited water, it will never be as beautiful as it could be with the right amounts of those essentials. Perhaps it may only ever be a seed—something with the potential to be beautiful and magnificent, but never amounting to anything but what simply could have been. I know The Friend spoke with you about the parable of the sower and how important the right soil is.

"Buddy, I want to remind you that what you learn on The River is preparing your soil; it is cultivating your heart so that you can sprout into that magnificence that I want you to become. Without this River, Buddy, you will never know your true purpose and become that which will eternally fulfill you."

Buddy suddenly felt enlightened—he got it. Yes, he had understood The Friend and the parable of the sower, but just now, he got it. It made total sense to him, and the fact that he was actually created to be something beautiful and magnificent? Well, his manly emotions (or suppressed emotions) had kept that from sinking in before. He was meant to be magnificent.

Wow, Buddy thought, *beautiful and magnificent*. As feminine as he thought those words were before, they now took on a more majestic and purposeful feeling— a feeling of worth, and being special and intended for something special, instead of haphazardly living for some superficial goals. Everything he was ever taught before had told him that he was chaotically placed on this earth for some random "unpurpose," probably to make money and do good, but other than that, there was no real ambition, and definitely no eternal purpose involving any kind of magnificence.

"Magnificent," Buddy said again.

The Guide smiled and softly chuckled, this time audibly, and said to Buddy, "Pretty cool, eh, Buddy?"

Buddy felt almost royal, and The Guide, still smiling, put His arm around Buddy and walked him to The River's edge. The Guide told Buddy to inspect the back side of the canoe before he set off, and Buddy walked over and immediately fell to his knees. To his absolute amazement, in the same manner that his name was etched into the front side of the canoe, he found that on the back side of the canoe was etched, *Magnificent*.

He incessantly ran his fingers over the etching, and then he looked up through tearing eyes at The Guide, who was still smiling. Buddy couldn't explain the magnitude of his emotions, but he knew, beyond the shadow of a doubt, that he was where he was supposed to be.

CHAPTER 7

The Push Off

*"The Christian experience, from start to finish,
is a journey of faith."*
– Watchman Nee

By this time, Buddy felt emotionally wrecked. But the peace of knowing that he was, for the first time in his life, exactly where he was supposed to be gave him strength, and the ability to take another step and get prepared to launch into the unknown. The Guide walked up to Buddy, looked him deep in the eyes, and said, "You're ready, Buddy."

Buddy said, "Really? Because I don't know if I can do this. I mean, I feel different, and I know that this is where I'm supposed to be. I trust You and I trust my Friend, but I don't know whether I am too weak for this. Look at me—I am far from magnificent, and right now I feel like the only thing I have to offer is being weak."

The Guide, with His now somewhat common smile, looked at Buddy and said, "You are definitely ready, and I'm a pretty good judge of character."

The Guide went on to explain a simple but fundamental truth to Buddy. "Buddy, you are what The Friend says you are. You are how The Friend sees you. He bestowed the word magnificent on you because that is how He sees you. Do you have faults? Yes. Do you fail more times than you succeed right now? Yes. But The Friend looks at the heart. He sees you as you can be and treats you as such. You are what The Friend says you are. The more you read The Book, the more you will see that your identity lies not in what you see but in what He sees. Buddy, claim your name: Magnificent; claim your identity."

Buddy didn't know how to respond. It seemed simple, but he didn't really understand how to believe it. He began thinking about how he'd always seen his own value and identity based on his successes and failures, on whether he was liked or disliked by certain people. It was a moving baseline that never seemed to go above mediocre.

"Do you trust Me, Buddy?" asked The Guide.

Buddy snapped to and thought that he wanted to shake his head in disagreement, because a nod of agreement would send him on an unknown voyage into who knows what, and he genuinely felt ill-equipped.

But Buddy, with the slight vigor he felt left in his heart, nodded in agreement.

"Alrighty then, Buddy, you are about to embark on the greatest voyage known to man, and it's tailored specifically and intentionally just for you. There is no luck, chance, or room for skepticism. There is only room for faith, hope, trust, and magnificence," said The Guide.

Finally, The Guide motioned for Buddy to get into the canoe. As Buddy scanned his surroundings to get acclimated to it all, he noticed that where the word *Magnificent* was etched so beautifully into the canoe, it read the same on the inside, but not backwards. It was situated so that he could read it as often as he looked at it.

The Guide leaned closer to Buddy as He began to push him off and said in his ear,

"I thought you might like to read that from in here as well. You may need to be reminded of who you are occasionally. Okay now, Buddy, do you have everything you need?"

Buddy looked around and said sarcastically, "I know I'm new to this, but a paddle would come in handy right about now." The Voice walked up and they all chuckled. Buddy gave a nervous laugh, because he figured The Voice had made a little oversight and just forgotten to give him a paddle. The Voice and The Guide laughed because they knew that was what Buddy was thinking.

Buddy felt that The Voice was more than just a voice at this point. He felt a familiarity and trust that was more like that of a Friend and less like just a voice.

"Well, Buddy, actually there is no paddle for you yet," The Friend said.

"Imagine that," Buddy said. "That will be interesting."

"I don't know about interesting, but I know it will be challenging, yet freeing," The Friend said.

"Um, freeing me to crash into the rock in the middle of The River? That doesn't sound like too much fun," Buddy said, still in his sarcastic mode—half joking, half serious.

"It's not all about fun, Buddy. This trip will have some fun times, but this process is mainly about breaking you of old, faith-crushing habits and attitudes, and replacing them with habits and attitudes that will make you a conqueror who is victorious in the challenges you face."

"But how do I navigate away from obstacles and hazards in The River?" Buddy inquired.

"You mean, how do you avoid challenges that you see coming ahead of you?" The Friend asked.

"Precisely," Buddy said with a sense of relief that The Friend finally understood his fear.

"Well, this is our first task, Buddy. I do not want you to spend time worrying about what is ahead, about avoiding obstacles or hazards in your way. If you continually worry about navigating your own way, you will never be still enough to grasp My way. You see, the only way for Me to begin to help you to follow Me is to remove your ability to navigate. Once you freely relinquish this ability, you are in line with My will for you. You are allowing Me to show you My path for you while you allow yourself to trust Me. Trust that whatever way you flow down that River is the way I have set for you, and that I am with you," The Friend said with purpose. "Until you voluntarily relinquish that right, you will not be in line with My will for you and this journey."

The Friend continued, "Where would you be if I gave you a paddle right away?"

Buddy replied, "I would be wherever I wanted to be."

"Exactly, Buddy, wherever you navigated yourself to. The point of this journey is for you to learn how to trust Me and not yourself. If I gave you a paddle, this would be about you navigating through something in your own ability. Haven't you done that enough? You don't need more obstacles where you can solve a problem, or find a solution, or navigate through a tricky situation. You need for Me to show you that I am capable, and that I want to put you on a certain path—a path only meant for you, that will bring you to the place that aligns your desires with Mine. I don't need you to prove yourself to Me right now, Buddy. I need to prove Myself and My ways to you, so that you can trust Me with greater and greater things, both on and off this River, and to the places beyond.

"I know this is a lot for you to take in right now, but trust Me that I know what is best for you. I know that the way for our desires to be aligned is for you to trust Me and allow Me to prove Myself to you. Don't get Me wrong, Buddy—I do not need to prove Myself to anyone, ever. But I want to prove Myself to you, so you can understand that I am worthy of your trust. Once you see Me providing for you and navigating you to specific places in specific times, you will never want to trust yourself again, only Me.

"That is where I want you to be—the place where you trust Me more than you trust yourself. One day I will give you challenges and tasks that will require hard work from you, work that I give you, and work that will require tools like a paddle. But until then, discard the desire to navigate yourself and allow Me to navigate your path," The Friend concluded.

"Um, so I guess I don't want a paddle—and I guess I have everything I need, so I'm ready," Buddy said, half sure.

As The Friend pushed Buddy off into the middle of The River, He gave Buddy one more suggestion. "If I were you, I would take this time to embrace the simplicity of the situation and concentrate on trusting Me. Do this by combating every doubt that arises in your head every time a doubt enters your brain. Replace it with Me telling you that I am trustworthy, and that this is the only way you will get to your destiny. Do not allow those negative, untrusting thoughts to have any control or influence. Make sure you combat them with truth—My truth. My truth is this, Buddy: I know what is best for you. I will not harm you, and I will direct your paths in complete perfection, crafting you into the person you were meant to be. So, even when it seems ridiculous to trust Me, do it anyway. I will not be proven wrong... ever.

"There is a passage in The Book that I want to give to you for this very purpose. 'The Lord is my shepherd, I shall not want. He makes me lie down in green pastures; He leads me beside quiet waters. He restores my soul; He guides me in the paths of righteousness for His name's sake. Even though I walk through the valley of the shadow of death, I fear no evil, for You are with me; Your rod and Your staff, they comfort me.'[11] Memorize that, Buddy, for every time you begin to fear or doubt. There will be times you are even tempted to doubt My very existence.

"As you drift down The River, lie down and spread your arms out and let Me take you to where you need to be—and remember, Buddy, trust Me. Read your journal every day and remember what I told you: that you

---

11 Psalm 23:1-4 NASB

were made for a purpose, and I will bring you to where you need to be, right when you need to be there. No one else can do that for you—no one. Regardless of what they want you to think, or what they try to convince you of, they can't deliver what I can... your destiny!

"You won't always have this opportunity to be at total rest and just sit back and let The River flow. There will be many times when you will be working hard to accomplish those things that I will put in your path. So, relax, and take in this precious time of just watching Me. Get to know Me and My ways better with every bend in The River. Embrace this time and let it start to change you, and change your belief in Me from something that is a myth and a legend to something that is real and right at your doorstep, beckoning to be known better by you. I want to be the Lord of your life—not a passenger or bystander, but the navigator who brings you to your pure, right, and perfect existence.

"Remember, Buddy, that I will never force you to love or trust Me. I will always be there with My hand outstretched, waiting for you to want to trust Me. I am telling you that trusting Me is the best option for you, and that only through wholeheartedly trusting Me will you be able to reach your destiny. But whether you choose to trust Me is always up to you. It is a continuous choice that you must make each day. The Destroyer knows that trust is the key to our relationship, and if he can deter you from trusting Me by whatever means necessary, you will not know Me and will never have a full and rewarding relationship with Me.

"That is what The Deceiver wants. I want you to trust Me, and he wants you to trust yourself. It's a choice, but My hope is that you will trust Me. Don't forget—if you fail, I will be here with outstretched arms to take you back... always.

"Know that I hear you, that I am not someone far off but One who is near you. I oblige when Seekers ask Me to guide their life's path. The struggle begins when I direct their path in a specific course and they fight that change because it's uncomfortable, or not exactly what they want. The struggle gets tougher and tougher when they fight what I've put in their path. It leads to frustration, depression, and anxiety. Let Me guide you; let go and trust Me."

As Buddy lay down in his canoe, his mind began to peacefully wander off with excitement for what lay ahead of him on The River. He slowly forgot about the absence of a paddle, as well as the rapids he had been shown earlier in the day. He simply embraced the moment and the ability to be serenely guided down The River. As his mind wandered, he imagined what his future would look like. He wanted to know what the details would be, and exactly what lessons and character surgery would manifest itself. But for now, for the first time in his life, Buddy knew he was where he was supposed to be, and he was at total peace.

CHAPTER 8

On the River

*"But God doesn't call us to be comfortable. He calls us
to trust Him so completely that we are unafraid to put
ourselves in situations where we will be in trouble if He
doesn't come through."*
– Francis Chan

Buddy lay in the canoe, watching the tree limbs sway in the warm breeze, the sun casting rays of sunlight all around The River. He relaxed in the moment, remembering all the things that his new Friend had told him. He began to wonder who The Friend really was. Was He more than an expert river guide and spiritual guru? Or was there no more to Him than what He had revealed to Buddy? He was hoping that one day he would be able to converse with his Friend again, in as intimate a way as he had done just now.

Lying peacefully and floating down The River, thoroughly enjoying the moment, brought Buddy into a calm peace. It felt as though he had been drifting effortlessly for hours and hours when suddenly, he was jolted violently out of the canoe. It began filling with water and was now half submerged.

Buddy came up out of The River and gasped for breath. He was angry that something had broken up his peaceful floating, and scared that he might drown. Immediately, he began wondering if all that he had believed would happen on The River—that The Friend would protect him—had been just a lie. As his thoughts ran wild, he felt a huge thud as his head hit the large rock in the middle of The River. Everything went dark, and Buddy was unconscious.

* * *

His vision came back to him very slowly as he began to focus on the image of a person he did not know. He found that it took a few minutes to even get a word out of his mouth. He finally muttered, "Wait... what... I don't remember..."

"Rest," the woman said to him gently. She continued tending to him with gentle yet seemingly proficient hands.

He quickly felt his eyelids get heavy, and once again everything went dark. After some time, he awoke once more. He was unable to recognize where he was but noticed that it was getting dark. He sat for a few minutes, trying to get a handle on his whereabouts and what he was doing there. Suddenly, he thought that he had obviously been misguided and couldn't really trust someone else to take the reins and guide him through anything. It was up to him to make his own way, and to find a way off this River and get back to what he knew. His dissatisfaction and disappointment began to fester and grow with every thought that entered his head.

He was now awake and alert, and said to the woman, "Thanks for helping me. I'm not sure what happened, but I need to find a way to either get down The River or get back to where I started at The River's edge, so I can go back to where I'm from."

"Wow, that was quick," she said. "You've been on The River—what, an hour or two, and now you're done? I'm Helper, and it's a good thing I was here when you needed someone."

Before Buddy could excuse himself, Helper continued. "You've been floating down this River for just a little while, and at the first sign of trouble, you're outta here?"

Buddy began his defense. "Well, I was told that all I had to do was float down The River and The Voice would guide me to where I needed to be. How did that work out? My head feels like it's going to explode, and I think I just drank half The River, so let me ask you: How am I doing? Am I where I am supposed to be?"

As Buddy uttered these words, he felt his old sense of sarcasm return with a vengeance. He was amazed at how easily those words flowed out of his mouth.

"Well, if The Voice told you to trust Him, and that He would lead you to where you need to be, then He did," Helper suggested.

"Okay, so why am I here?" Buddy asked sarcastically.

"All I know is that my Friend asked me to come by here today at 3 p.m. I did, because I know that if He asks me to go, I go. I know that I may not understand why, but I do understand who asked me. The why will come later. The who is what is important. There have been many people in my life whom I have tried to trust with all my heart, and I was let down. But I know that if I am asked anything by my Friend, it is for a purpose, and I do it.

"Why are you here? I don't know for sure, but I suppose maybe that's why," Helper said, pointing down-river at a shadowy figure in a canoe going against the stream. "I think that's part of the reason, and it may be that you were not ready to meet him yet."

Buddy did not know what to say. He noticed that the person in the canoe was scouring The River for something, as if he were expecting something to be there and it wasn't.

"Who is that?" Buddy asked sheepishly.

"Oh, well, that's The Destroyer. He rides up and down The River, searching to undo and misdirect," the Helper said sternly, as if she had some experience with him.

"Um, how do I avoid him?" Buddy asked.

"You don't. He is always there, waiting to strike, but the good thing about him is that all he has is a roar. He is powerless, except for that which you give him power over. You see, he cannot take what you do not give him. He will try to deceive and destroy you, to make you fail on this River and go back to being what you were. But if you stand strong on everything that The Friend told you, you will make it.

"Buddy, I know why you needed rescuing from The River," Helper said.

"Okay, tell me," Buddy said curiously.

"Well, as you may have noticed, I have been down this River before. I wasn't perfect in every trial that came my way, but I learned. I absorbed more each time I failed and each time I had success. I made it to the Waterfall, and then The Friend told me to come here. I was disappointed, because I had made it all the way down The River in one piece and accomplished the task. I thought there would be some mighty revelation or some epiphany about where I was to go from there. In my frustration and doubt, I so quickly forgot about all the things my Friend had shown me and brought me through on my River. I forgot those things and began to doubt the purpose for all of it—until now, that is."

"Okay, so you helped me out of the water, and now you understand everything?" Buddy asked.

"No, Buddy, not quite. You see, I still had the question of what I should do with my life. I had given it all over to The Friend and was waiting to see what He would give back to me. Until today, I did not know what that would be. He told me a few days ago, 'You will know what I have for you when it is before you.' I thought it sounded a little vague, but I am learning to trust, even when I have doubts. When I was tending to you on The River, I knew I had something to offer. I felt alive and useful. I have gone through so many things in my life where I felt nominal and ordinary, just one of the crowd. Yet today, when I helped you out of The River and nursed you back to health, I felt alive, and I heard my Friend's words repeated in my soul. 'You will know what I have for you when it is before you.'

"I am a helper, a servant to those who are in anguish and need. I have a lot to offer because of all that my Friend has done for me. Buddy, you came here to help me. As ironic as that sounds, it's true."

"Happy to help," Buddy said awkwardly, since he really didn't know what to say, because he really hadn't done anything.

He suddenly felt a little special. It began to hit him. Maybe this was real. If he had a paddle, he would have navigated around the big rock and met The Destroyer, which gave him the creeps, and he would have missed Helper altogether. The thought crossed his mind that if he had somehow seen the big rock and avoided it, The Friend would have sent someone else for the Helper to mend.

But the fact that he was in the equation made him feel unique and special. It appeared that there was a reason for all of this. And when something has a reason, it is important. He felt as though he was on the cusp of something profound. Then, he wondered how many of these opportunities he had neglected or overlooked in his life so far. How many times was he meant to be used for a purpose, and he had complained and whined about a situation rather than trying to see the reasons for it? He could have been trying to find answers and meaning, rather than running away from problems and working himself out of them. He rarely, if ever, paused to find out why.

Helper could see that Buddy was deep in thought, so once she noticed that he had made eye contact again with her, she resumed explaining. "There are two philosophies that people adopt here on The River and beyond. The first is a theory that pretty much says that we are out here on our own, for the most part. We are here and anything we need, we must make happen on our own, for ourselves. The Friend was there to lead us in the beginning; however, He watches us from a distance, and judges us based upon what we do with what we have.

"The other philosophy is more personal. It suggests that The Friend is concerned with every step we take. He desires to help navigate every single decision in our life. He wants to direct us and guide us through each decision to bring us to the exact place He has destined for us. He uses some of the truths written in The Book to guide us. He also uses fresh, new words personalized for us. Even when He uses words that have been written in The Book to guide us, He wants us to seek Him at every step. This builds a relationship. I know you are fresh on The River, and I also know that The Guide will be talking to you and reminding you about relationships repeatedly. So, for now, just know that The Friend desires to fulfill that name, 'Friend,' with you."

After Helper was finished, she simply walked a few steps backwards and said, "Remember, Buddy, seek and find. And thanks for the part you played in my journey. I know that you would rather see yourself as an island and not need anyone else's help or guidance. But I want you to know that The Friend intends for us Seekers to help, love, and consider each other. The better you understand that, the better you will meet The Friend's call to love and serve others, and the closer you'll come to Him." With that, Helper smiled, then turned around and walked away with a skip in her step.

As Helper walked away, Buddy noticed that he had new hope in The Friend. He remembered speaking with The Friend on The River's edge, when he only knew Him as The Voice. That was an exciting time, and he remembered His voice and the things He had said. But now, seeing The Friend work in real life, directing his path and navigating him to the exact place He wanted Buddy to go—well, it was amazing, even supernatural. This is what he had thought it would be like when he had first made the Decision, before he knew anything about The River.

He supposed that a lack of discipleship and mentoring had probably hurt him on his journey. He had never really wanted anyone's help. He had spent most of his life being let down and disappointed, which made him rely upon himself and no one else. The whole thing about trusting and "having community" with other Seekers did not make him feel as warm and fuzzy as becoming closer to The Friend. He thought that he had spent so long not wanting to trust or rely on people that this might be a tough road ahead.

So, Buddy moved that thought to the back of his mind and continued dwelling on how awesome it was to know that The Friend was showing such interest and placing such value on his journey.

Noticing that it was dark now, he decided to rest there for the night so that he could be ready for the next morning. Then he remembered the two theories that Helper had spoken about, so he lay down and simply spoke out loud, as if The Friend were there, listening.

"I'm not sure if I should stay here and camp for the night, or if I should keep going. I realized today that everything You said is real, and I want to trust You and keep in line with the exact road You have ordained for me. Can You let me know if I should stay or if I should go?" As Buddy spoke out loud, he felt a little ridiculous about speaking to someone who was not physically in front of him.

He began to walk around the immediate area and he heard a still, small voice in his head: *Rest and read.* Buddy had a hard time differentiating his own inner voice from the possibility of something or someone else speaking to his mind. It was a bit eerie, but kind of cool too. He figured that it was the best he had to go on, so he decided to stay there and rest.

As he sat down, he heard in his head: Read. And he suddenly remembered that The Voice in his head had said to rest and read. Then he began remembering that he was told to read The Book in the morning and the evening. He wanted to make sure he was doing his part along the way. So, he opened The Book to an arbitrary page and read this, "Come to Me, all who labor and are heavy laden, and I will give you rest. Take My yoke upon you, and learn from Me, for I am gentle and lowly in heart, and you will find rest for your souls. For My yoke is easy, and My burden is light."[12]

Buddy remembered that he had read something similar on the log he had sat down to rest on as he was taking a jog. He remembered that he had felt such a peace from simply reading that, and he knew that this would somehow be an important milestone in his new journey.

---

12 Matthew 11:28-30 ESV

Flowing Together

"You must learn to be strong in the dark as well as in the day, else you will always be only half brave."
– George MacDonald

As Buddy woke up from a very deep and energizing sleep, he suddenly recognized that he was quite hungry. He began to look around, as it was getting lighter. He noticed a bush with some berries on it, so he took some and brought them back to where he had slept. There was an eagerness inside of him to read The Book because of how applicable it was to him the last time he had read it. He knew now that what he read at the beginning of each day would be relevant to what he would soon encounter. It might also be a reflection on something he had just experienced. So, he deduced that what he read this morning would be a part of what he would experience soon enough. He read with expectancy, and turned to a page that spoke about "taking every thought captive."[13] That seemed foreign to him, and also seemed like a lot of work.

Being refreshed from a restful sleep, and having gathered some delicious berries for his stomach as well as some food for thought, he was ready to set out on The River a second time. He dragged his canoe from the bank of The River, jumped in, and set off expectantly. He was pondering about Helper and all she had done—her timing and her care. He began to recollect and marvel at the fact that the canoe flipping—and his almost drowning, as well as being cared for by Helper—had allowed him to escape The Deceiver. He was curious about The Deceiver and why he was there, and what he could possibly want with him. After all, it's not like he was anyone special. Also, he had never really had many serious confrontations with anyone, so it couldn't have been a vengeance thing. The creepiness and slyness of The Deceiver gave Buddy chills as he remembered seeing him searching The River as he slithered by. Regardless of what The Deceiver wanted with him, he was glad to have avoided that encounter and he hoped that, if possible, he would never make his acquaintance—but somehow, he felt it would be inevitable.

Buddy was still awestruck that the timing of everything was so bizarre. He remembered feeling a new level of importance once he realized how almost perfect the

13 2 Corinthians 10:5

timing was. It seemed purposeful. He wondered how much was coincidence, and how much was intentional. Not that he doubted Helper's interpretation, but he had known some people before who seemed to always think everything happened for a reason. He wasn't one of them. To Buddy, when things worked out in his favor it was more of a coincidence and something haphazard, rather than something that had any specific intent or significance behind it. And as much as he told himself that coincidence was probably the case, he couldn't help but wonder if he had it all wrong in his mind. Because if the latter were true and it was all purposeful, then things *do* happen for a reason, and the next logical conclusion would be to search for those reasons. But maybe he'd get some epiphany on this issue another time, because now he was pushing off for another day of adventure on the water.

Even though Buddy was still paddleless, he felt a simplicity and a comfort with the fact that he could relax and let The River navigate his journey. There were little paths and currents that he thought would make more sense to follow, but for the most part, he was letting go and letting The River take him where he needed to be. After all, if there was a chance that all of this was destined for him—to go down a certain specific route—even the slight chance that this was true was enough to let go and keep on track, whatever track that was. If there was a chance that he was destined for something special and could possibly become something magnificent, he had to try. As the sun shone through the trees, he marveled at the beauty of the water passing by and the splendor all around him.

As Buddy scanned the riverbank on either side, he noticed a lot of paths that seemed to lead from The River's edge to a wooded path that led into a deeper forest, much like the path he had followed when he first heard The Voice. As he drifted closer to some of these paths, he noticed that many of them were overgrown, and some even had canoes that were lined up but overrun with vines and branches. It looked as if no one had been there in quite some time. As he drifted by one of the overgrown paths, he could almost see down about ten or fifteen yards of the path, and he wondered how anyone could even see The River from the path. It was as if it were being hidden purposely.

"Hey, you!" A voice shouted and startled Buddy so much that he almost tipped his canoe. Buddy turned around to see a very confident man canoeing toward him.

With his stomach still feeling like it was in his throat from being so frightened, he said, "You scared me."

To that, Striver responded, "If you weren't so distracted with those paths, you might have heard me coming."

Buddy didn't know if that was an insult or just simply an observation, but either way, he wasn't too enamored with the comment. It made him feel as if this guy were intentionally trying to make him feel a bit dim.

Striver asked Buddy what he was doing there, and why he was taking so long getting down The River. Buddy explained that he had recently begun his journey down The River and that he had been instructed to just let The River guide him to where he should go.

Striver sort of snickered at Buddy and said, "Oh, yes, I remember that 'beginner stage' of the game; it seems like so long ago. You know, many people never get a paddle to use, because they don't reach the point where they can handle the responsibility or the challenge. But as you can see, I have a beautiful paddle that allows me to navigate wherever I choose on this River. I would not give this beauty up for anything."

Buddy had just met Striver and already didn't care for him too much. He understood the wisdom in the saying not to judge a book by its cover, but somehow it seemed reasonable to "judge away" in this case.

Trying not to sound too interested in what Striver was saying, but not intending to be rude either, Buddy replied, "Yes, I can't wait until I finally get my paddle; it will be much easier to get around."

Striver shrugged his shoulders as if to say, "That's nice, but if you're not going to marvel at my paddle anymore, I'm outta here."

Buddy's face was now surely showing some contempt as he thought, *I mean, it's a nice paddle, but that dude needs to get over himself.*

Striver looked at Buddy and said with his own dose of sarcasm, "Well, I hope you have fun floating. I've got to run, so good luck and happy drifting."

Striver splashed Buddy, which he was sure was purposeful, but Striver never looked back to apologize. Somehow, Buddy knew that Striver was so unpleasant and pious that he was sure to run into him again.

As Buddy continued to float down The River, happy that he could once more enjoy The River without the annoyance of that arrogant guy, he decided to lie back and enjoy the silence. He began to wonder, though, why a guy like that could be trusted with a paddle, but he couldn't. *I mean, surely I could be more courteous and responsible than that guy.*

As Buddy relaxed in the canoe, he began feeling a tad inadequate, as if there could be something wrong with him. Perhaps he didn't have a paddle because he wouldn't ever have one, because he couldn't handle one in the eyes of The Friend. As these thoughts crept into his mind, he remembered the verse from this morning—taking every thought captive.

He found himself in the midst of a struggle that was also making him envious of Striver. *Why would that guy be given the privilege of a paddle, and why can he float around at will and I can't?* Buddy began to wonder. *If I could only have what he has, I could do so much more than he would.* These thoughts swam around again in his head and became darker and harder to dismiss with every second, clouding his mind with envy and thoughts of inadequacy as he yearned for what Striver had.

Then, amid his mental dilemma, alongside his canoe a familiar face rowed closer to him; it was The Guide. He remembered that The Friend had told him that The Guide would be along from time to time to instruct him in the ways of The River. Man, was it good to see Him.

"So, where are you, Buddy?" The Guide asked directly. At once, Buddy remembered that question from when The Friend had asked it of him. He suddenly realized that the place he was drifting toward in his head was a distraction, and it was causing him to move farther away from where he should be.

"Buddy, right now is such an important time in many ways for you," The Guide said softly, yet passionately. "The habits you form on this River and the lessons you learn will dictate much of your future. If you are pliable, humble, and learn to keep growing, you will find that your life makes sense. Even in situations that the average person would question and doubt, you will perceive the higher purpose and enjoy the fruits of a deeper walk with your Friend and an understanding of The Creator. If you listen for My prompting and advice, you will become secure and strong. Even more so in the times when you feel weakest; you will get stronger because you trust in what I tell you.

"You will seek My counsel, and I will give it to you. In each situation where you look for My perspective, you will trust Me more and recognize My voice, even and especially when you don't see Me, Buddy. What you are going through at this very moment will help to shape who you become. You have a choice. You can either give in to the dark and deceitful thoughts in your head, or you can combat them with truth. It is not enough to simply reject the dark thoughts that pop up in your head. It is required that you purge from your mind the dark thoughts and replace them with truth.

"You are in a battle. Mental battles are sometimes the toughest battles we face. It will take every ounce of strength to fight the attacks. Your default reaction to dark thoughts will be to entertain them or to do nothing; each of those options will lead you to defeat. Fight, Buddy! Do you know what combats the darkness every time? The light does. When you are in a dark room and you need to see something, you turn on the light, and the darkness vanishes. Each time you do battle with those dark thoughts, you need light. The Book and the truths within are the light you need to defeat the darkness.

"Remember that no one can make you angry, envious, or inadequate. Don't give that right to anyone. No one can make you angry, Buddy, but you can allow their actions or words to make you angry. Never give that away. Remember, it's a fight!

"You experienced two specific attacks just now. First, you allowed the fact that Striver had a paddle to make you envious. You envied a gift that The Friend had given to someone else. You assumed that either The Friend had made a mistake in not giving you a paddle, or that you knew better than He. Either way, Buddy, you presumed too much.

"When you begin to question the wisdom of The Friend compared with your own, remember and continually tell yourself this quote from The Book: 'For My thoughts are not your thoughts, nor are your ways My ways, declares The Creator. For as the heavens are higher than the earth, so are My ways higher than your ways and My thoughts than your thoughts.'[14] Recite this and believe it, and watch those dark thoughts of questioning The Friend's wisdom flee from your mind as you win the battle. Do not submit to the lies you hear.

---

14 Isaiah 55:8-9 NASB

"The other area that started you on your mental voyage of inadequacy was that you somehow believed it was a matter of Seekers deserving the paddle, or another tool meant to be a blessing. In reality, it is grace that determines who receives what. If you have not received something that you think you need, it may in fact be that you are simply not ready to receive it. There is more that The Friend must show you and teach you before you can properly use the gift. Do not let anyone convince you, or let any thought creep into your head saying that it is an issue of deserving something. For Seekers do not deserve; they are given by grace the things they need or righteously desire.

"The Destroyer will use all sorts of mental attacks to attempt to make you believe that it is simply due to your inadequacy or a fault in you that you do not have what other people have. If there is a fault within you, The Friend will help you correct it and move on, but feelings of inadequacy from not getting what you think you deserve are born from useless guilt. Guilt without My prompting is in vain; guilt with My prompting convicts the heart and leads to change.

"Change makes you stronger, Buddy. It is your friendship and ongoing relationship with The Friend that make you adequate. When The Creator of all looks upon you to judge, He sees The Friend, who stands in the gap for you, and He therefore judges you based upon who The Friend is, since you abide in Him—not on any accomplishments or character traits within yourself. Remember, you are with Him; He is not with you. If The Friend leads and you are by His side, you will succeed. If you expect to lead and hope that The Friend will follow you, you will fail and be frustrated.

"Bottom line is this: You will undergo more damaging mental attacks than physical ones, regardless of the severity of any physical attack you could sustain. Therefore, if anyone is in The Friend, he is a new creation. The old has passed away; behold, the new has come."[15] First, memorize this verse, and then have it at your ready and recite it as soon as you recognize the mental attack or feelings of inadequacy. Basically, The Friend is telling you that once you were inadequate, but the day you decided to be His friend, you were more than adequate; you were transformed (and you continue to be transformed) into being more like The Friend with every breath you take. That is where you want to be. Being in the right place—your destiny—is more of a state of mind and a state of character than it is a physical place or time; never forget that, Buddy. In the midst of these mental battles, focus on what really matters: who you are, not what you do.

"The Book is full of wisdom and truth; use it as a sword to fight on your side during these battles of the

---

15 2 Corinthians 5:17 ESV (replaced Christ with Friend)

mind. Remember this next saying from The Book as soon as you recognize thoughts that come from anything or anyone other than Me or The Friend: 'We destroy arguments and every lofty opinion raised against the knowledge of The Friend, and take every thought captive to obey The Friend...'[16] This quote explains so well the tool that you must use in order to be more like The Friend—taking every thought captive. Not *some* thoughts, but every thought. Take captive every thought that stands in opposition to what The Friend has told you. Fight it off with truth, Buddy, and you will succeed."

The Guide went on to tell Buddy how he must treat every situation as a learning experience.

"You must begin to analyze situations," The Guide stated. "You have to analyze your situation to get to know yourself better than you do today. It is of utmost importance to know yourself and your tendencies better; only then you can know exactly how to arm yourself. If you can figure out some of your more frequent and destructive tendencies, then you will know how to fight the mental battles that accompany them.

"What is the mental struggle you fight most often? Is it a feeling of depression, anxiousness, inadequacy, jealousy, envy, pride, or anger? Find passages from The Book that help combat those lies. Discover your men-

---

16 2 Corinthians 10:5 ESV (replaced Christ with Friend)

tal tendencies and learn how to battle them. Once you begin to have success in combating those larger issues, you can begin to tackle the smaller or less frequent ones. But it is a constant battle; one victory does not mean you have won the war. The war is ongoing, and both large and small battles can emerge or reemerge at any time, so you must be on guard."

Buddy almost forgot where he was for a moment. As he sat drifting along The River, his mind began to explode with thoughts and pictures about all the times he had let unhealthy thoughts enter his head and change his feelings, which in turn changed the steps he took in his life. Actually, fighting these thoughts seemed foreign to him, and he soon realized why he had lost just about every mental battle he had been involved in up to this point. He had let unhealthy thoughts rule his mind and then dictate his actions. Buddy had not realized how active this life with The Friend really was; it was not a passive life at all. It was an active lifestyle of battles and victories that would lead him to successfully transform into his destiny. As he floated down The River, he felt inspired and almost excited to face the next mental battle. Little did Buddy know that the next mental battle would come sooner than he thought.

As Buddy and The Guide parted ways, The Guide said that the more Buddy took time to listen to The Guide, the more he would recognize The Guide and His instructions. But He mentioned to Buddy that this too was a process; getting to learn how to hear The Guide was an art. Like all relationships, it would take time, patience, and persistence.

The Guide said, "Think of our relationship like any other relationship you have. The more time you spend with someone, the more you get to know them. The more you get to know them, the richer and deeper that relationship becomes. Remember to listen. Also, like other relationships, if you continue to do all the talking, you will not hear what the other person has to say. The words I speak are life to you, Buddy, and you must remember to do yourself a favor and show Me the respect I deserve and listen more than you speak. That little bit of advice will do wonders for your journey."

As the day turned into evening and the sky grew darker, Buddy found his canoe drifting toward a flattened area by The River's edge. As his canoe drifted toward the bank, Buddy thought it was kind of cool how it must have been The Friend directing his canoe, as if saying that the day was finished. Buddy unloaded his canoe, set up camp, and after fetching some dinner from the native plants and fruit trees, he lay down and took out The Book and began reading.

He opened up to a verse that read, "It is good to give thanks to The Friend and to sing praises to [His] name... To declare [His] lovingkindness in the morning and [His] faithfulness by night, with the ten-stringed lute and with the harp, with resounding music upon the lyre."[17] Buddy read this and thought that the notion of praising something or someone seemed a little weird. For one, he did not have any musical instruments; and even if he had, as far as musical talents go, he was in short supply.

But there was something simplistic yet seemingly natural about doing this once he started. If he looked at it more simply, it could be just stating his thanks for what The Friend had done for him, and maybe even pre-thanking Him for the things He had yet to do. So, as Buddy put The Book down, he began quietly speaking to The Friend as if He were there with him. He offered up thanks about general things like letting him come on The River and guiding his way.

Then he found himself becoming more targeted in his thanks, for such things as the *Magnificent* carving and Helper. He even thought to thank The Friend for allowing his canoe to be upset in the water, so that Helper could come and feel more confident about herself. There was still something magical about the timing of the incident with Helper. He left off there, and as his eyes became too heavy to remain open, Buddy drifted off into a deep sleep.

---

17 Psalm 92:1-3 NASB (author paraphrase)

CHAPTER 10

Give or Get?

"Seek to give much—expect nothing."
– Jonathan Goforth

In the middle of the night, Buddy was awakened by The Voice—just The Voice though, no physical presence. He heard, "Buddy, will you give or will you get?" He could feel his heart beating extremely fast from being woken up so suddenly, and it took several minutes for him to calm down. Once his heart rate was a little more normal, he began to think about that question. "Will you give or will you get?" It could mean nothing, and he thought maybe it was the end of some dream he didn't quite remember. He drifted back to sleep, and awoke a few hours later with the sun shining on his face through the trees.

Buddy woke to the sounds of birds chirping and a warm breeze blowing across his face. *It's a wonderful way to wake up*, he thought. It was yet another instance in the past few days that he wished he could bottle up and save for later.

He decided to read the words spoken by The Guide earlier, and he picked up The Book and began reading, "There is therefore now no condemnation for those who are in The Friend."[18] He read a little further about the flesh versus the spirit.

He wasn't entirely sure what that was saying, but he got the gist of it. Listening to the flesh, or his own human nature, was not good, and listening to the Spirit, and that part of him that was renewed in The Friend, was better. One way was human, and the other was spiritual. This time, though, he felt like the passage was quite general and wondered how it would apply to him. He thought maybe it was just to be put into the back of his mind for another occasion when it might come in handy.

Buddy decided it was time to again set off on a new journey on The River. He excitedly pushed his canoe into the water as he wondered what adventure he would encounter today.

Hopeful that this day would be as exciting as the past few, Buddy drifted downriver and took in all the beauty that The River had to offer. He began thinking that this experience on The River was something that he wished for other people he knew—to be able to ride this River

---

18 Romans 8:1 ESV (replaced Christ Jesus with Friend)

and learn life lessons from The Friend and The Guide. Although it was not easy—sometimes scary, and other times uncomfortable—he believed that this was where everyone needed to be, to know their own destiny and to begin to build faith in The Friend.

If there was one person whom he wished it for the most, it would have to be his youngest sister. She was his half-sister, but he would never introduce her that way because he thought of her as a true sister. There was nothing "step," or removed, about her. Perhaps it was because he truly loved her and felt responsible to protect her. It was Buddy who had actually raised her, as well as her other sisters. Buddy was the eldest child and had a different father from his sisters.

Their parents were not bad by any means, but they were self-absorbed and had never made the extra effort to show the children that they were truly loved and special. Buddy made every effort to make his siblings feel important and cared for, because before his own father had passed away, that's how Buddy had felt. He thought it was wrong and unfortunate that these girls didn't feel the way he had felt when he was younger.

Since his sisters were often overlooked and forgotten by their parents, Buddy often was the one who showed up at their events—many times with homemade signs, cheering them on. And even though the signs were fairly cheesy and simple, as much as the girls mocked them, it did indeed make them feel special and loved.

Cheerful was the youngest, then came Funny, and the oldest was Smart. He had this special relationship with all of them, but lately, he hadn't been able to see them as much as he wanted to, between his job and not living in the same house anymore. Although he had stayed close to them, it wasn't quite equal to living in the same house. There had been a little less community with them since he had moved out about ten years ago.

Cheerful was the only one still living at home. He often took her out and still managed to cheer her on at every event she had. He felt that it was his duty—and he truly loved them all, but with Cheerful being a little younger, he felt she needed encouragement and a sense of worth a little more due to her slightly sensitive nature. She was mostly happy and loved to spread that cheer, but she tended to takes things that offended her to heart. This was something she and Buddy had many a conversation about.

Christmastime was always special for him because he would get such wonderful gifts from them all, but especially from Cheerful. It was as if she was giving gifts to a dear parent, not a half-brother. One year in particular stood out. As they were opening gifts, she had saved the last one for him. Everyone else had finished opening presents and began leaving the room as she motioned to Buddy to stay for a minute.

After everyone was gone, she had given him a locket (which at first seemed quite feminine). He had inspected it and given the old, "Oh man, that's awesome," and then he had politely thanked her for it. She had rolled her eyes as if expecting a little more of a reaction, so she came over to him and gently turned it over.

She had said, "I'm sorry, but this is the only one I could find, and it was perfect for you." As he inspected it further, he noticed that it was inscribed on the back: "For a special Dad, **Brother & Friend.**" The "brother and friend" part was etched roughly on there as a homemade, aftermarket addition.

"Buddy, you have made me who I am today with every cheesy sign, simple hug, and loving gesture," she had said. "Without you, I would not want to live." And as she motioned for him to open the locket, he had expected a picture, but instead saw a tiny poem that read, "Every tear you wiped, every time you made me laugh, and every day you are in my life, it's better. From your Cheerful, Smart, and Funny."

Though he was not an especially emotional person, Buddy had all of a sudden let out a strange hiccup, followed by another, followed by crying uncontrollably for a few minutes. After he had dried his eyes, Cheerful said with a sense of accomplishment, "Now, that's more like it."

And as she had left the room, Funny and Smart had come in and kissed him on the head and said they loved him. As Smart kissed him, she said that the locket was from all of them, and Funny kissed him and said jokingly, "Ya girl."

As they had walked out of the room, the only words he could muster were, "You're all worth it." He had sat in the room, now alone, and had started crying again, happy that he had made such an impact. But the three girls could tell it was a happy cry as they sat and watched him from the stairs and had given each other a three-way high five.

So, if he could have anyone on The River with him, yeah, it would be them, especially Cheerful.

* * *

He had never felt like such an emotional wreck since, until he had seen the word *Magnificent* written on his canoe yesterday. With emotions running deep, Buddy drifted down The River, reminiscing about his past and wondering how much more he could have offered the girls had he met The Friend sooner. As Buddy coasted downriver, he was glad that he knew The Friend today, feeling secure that he was in capable hands.

He suddenly realized that he hadn't eaten in a while and was beginning to get slight hunger pangs. Along

The River, Buddy noticed what looked like makeshift campsites along the riverbank. He saw people at some of the campsites, and other sites seemed as though they had been vacated for some time. He wondered about all the different people there and what their stories were. *Are they like me, new to The River, or have they been here for a long time?* Some were by themselves, and others were in groups.

Buddy wondered how many people were farther into the woods instead of close to The River's edge. As The River narrowed, and the edge became rockier and more difficult to access, he noted that it had been a while since he had seen anyone at the edge. Once The River opened and there was easier access to the shore, he noticed a girl on one side of The River, looking disappointed and obviously crying as she stared into The River. He thought she looked like she needed help.

What actually went through his mind was that he would bet that this girl didn't have the support he had given to his sisters. He wasn't sure where that came from, and he didn't intentionally think of his sisters, but nonetheless he was thinking that this girl was lacking something. He thought that he was pretty good at sincerely making people feel better about themselves.

But he thought he also needed to eat something. He figured he wouldn't be much use because he was starting to get some severe hunger pangs—and really, how well could he concentrate when he was so hungry? After all, Buddy was so new to The River, what help could he be? He floated right by her, gave her a friendly smile, and continued downriver. He figured that there would surely be other people coming after him down The River who could probably help her out just as well. So, he continued downriver, looking back to check the status of Disappointed and noticing that the current had picked up speed substantially.

As he floated rapidly downriver, he noticed a figure on the opposite side who looked familiar. As he got closer, he noticed that it was Helper! How glad was he to see her? He often thought about her and what a vital part she had been in the first lesson he had learned on The River. He had wondered how she was and if he would see her again.

As he got closer to Helper, he noticed that she had set up camp for someone, as if she were expecting company. So, he decided that maybe she was waiting for someone else. As happy as he was to see her, he pretended not to notice her and continued downriver. But the fact that he had no paddle did not come in handy right then, because he started to float right toward her. Buddy nonchalantly tried to paddle with his hands away from the shoreline where Helper was, but it didn't work.

Helper shouted out to Buddy, smirking, "Going somewhere?"

While she smiled, she motioned for him to come on over to her. His canoe pulled itself right up to the shoreline where Helper was standing. Buddy looked up at her and said,

"Expecting someone?"

She began walking toward the two plates of food she had set up around the fire and said, "Only you, Buddy—only you."

He wasn't sure whether he was so happy to see Helper because he had special feelings for her, or simply because she had been there at such an instrumental time for him on The River.

But either way, he felt less intimate with her when she said, "I wish this was a happier meeting, but it's not. I have something for you." She pulled out a sleek-looking paddle with his *Magnificent* name on it. But the name wasn't as bright and fire-laden as it had been written before.

When she handed it to him, Buddy looked at it with amazement and a sense of accomplishment and said, "Oh, man, that's so cool. I guess The Friend thinks I'm ready for this bad boy." *It's about time*, he thought, as he began thinking of all the places he could navigate to with this sweet paddle.

But Helper interrupted Buddy's excitement as she said, "Buddy, you're doing such a great job on The River and you've grown a lot in such a short time here, but The Friend wanted me to give this to you not because you are successful or worthy, but because you need it for a choice that is in front of you."

Buddy felt a sense of excitement and anticipation as he wondered what incredible journey the Helper was about to send him on in the name of The Friend. Buddy's mood began to change once the Helper started explaining it in more detail.

"What was on your mind today, Buddy? What things were you thinking about today before you came to me?" she asked.

"Well, today I started reading in The Book about the flesh and the spirit, and how being guided by the Spirit was beneficial to my walk with The Friend and good for my own wellbeing. And then, for some reason, I began to think about my sisters, and how much I hoped that one day they could be on The River too," Buddy explained.

"It sounds like you really care about your sisters, Buddy," Helper said. "What about Disappointed? What did you think when you saw her?"

Buddy suddenly felt a great sense of guilt and immediate remorse for not helping her out. Just as he was thinking that he would do better next time, Helper said to him, "So what do you think, Buddy?"

Ashamed at this point—both for the fact that he had missed an opportunity to help someone and that he looked extremely selfish and uncompassionate in front of Helper—Buddy replied, "I think I'm going to do better next time," with confidence and a hint of remorse, trying to brush it off.

To that, Helper promptly replied, "Okay, so, poor Disappointed—hopefully someone else will make it to her in time?"

Feeling even worse, Buddy said, "Oh, well, um, maybe The Friend or The Guide will send someone else to help her. I mean, it would be a tough go of it upstream, right?"

All Helper did was glance at the new paddle Buddy was still awkwardly caressing.

"Oh," Buddy replied. "I guess I get why I'm ready for this. Not because I am deserving, but because it is necessary for what I have to do." Already knowing where this was going, Buddy stood up with a sense of determination and direction and glanced back at Helper, waved, and said, "I hope I get to see you again."

Helper smiled, and with a hushed voice replied, "Me too."

As Buddy began rowing upstream, he was amazed at the pace at which he could paddle, even though it was upstream. But he soon forgot about the glory of the paddle once The River's current made it extremely laborious to maneuver upriver. He noticed he had begun to break a sweat and had never realized how humid it was. *Is this for real? Can there be no one else who is closer?* Buddy thought. After all, he was still very hungry and not feeling quite up to the task, and he started to ease up on the paddling.

Just then, he noticed a shadowy figure on shore with Disappointed. As he was floating back downriver, he saw that this figure was obviously talking to Disappointed from The River's edge as she walked slowly into The River, with a blank stare and tears in her eyes.

The more the figure motioned and spoke, the farther in she went. Just then, the mysterious figure looked directly at Buddy, which startled him. The shadowy figure, with a greasy smirk, looked him in the eyes and then slowly turned back, commencing his directions to Disappointed with a greater sense of urgency.

Buddy felt a sense of pride well up in him; he felt as though Disappointed was in obvious trouble but was oblivious to it. It appeared that the glance by the shadowy figure was meant to scare off Buddy. It would have, had he not just been humiliated in front of Helper.

He felt a sudden and deep compassion for Disappointed, as well as a fire in his heart to get to her before something terrible happened. The ground Buddy had lost by being indifferent was quickly made up through his newfound desire to get to Disappointed as soon as possible. Although his thoroughly sweat-drenched clothes would say differently, Buddy felt as though it took little effort when he was determined to do something.

As he got closer, he noticed that the shadowy figure's face now took on a wicked expression and became contorted as he looked again at Buddy, but now with much more of an angry glare.

Buddy fixed his eyes on The Deceiver and jumped out of his canoe as Disappointed was now neck deep in The River. As he desperately swam toward her, he noticed that she suddenly lost her footing because of the current and went under.

No way! Buddy thought. *There is no way that this ends here, like this.* Buddy went under and felt the pull of the current as she crashed into him under water. He managed to grab one of her arms and hook her underneath her armpit as he swam with all his might, pulling her as he went. He suddenly felt the riverbed underneath his feet and leaned back and walked his way to the shore, pulling Disappointed with him.

As he made his way to shore, he laid her down and noticed that she was just staring at him in amazement.

"Why did you do that?" she asked, almost annoyed. "It was almost over, and now I'm still here."

Buddy didn't know what to say. That was not quite the response he was expecting. He suddenly felt weak in the knees and collapsed in exhaustion. Lying on The River's edge, he looked over at Disappointed and said, "You are worth it."

He was almost as surprised as she was that those words came out of his mouth. Buddy stared at Disappointed, and she turned away and started weeping.

Buddy lay there until Disappointed softened her crying and eventually lay silent. Once she was quiet, Buddy asked in a soft voice, "Who was speaking to you on The River's edge when you were walking into the water?"

Disappointed turned toward him and with a bewildered look replied, "What do you mean? No one was with me."

Buddy quickly responded, "Someone was on The River's edge, motioning for you to go farther into The River."

As she turned back away from Buddy, Disappointed said, "I'm not sure what you're talking about."

He could tell she wanted to be left alone for a bit, and Buddy quietly obliged. It seemed to him that hours passed as they lay there. He began looking around The River's edge and noticed that there was a canoe in the woods. It was old and rustic-looking, as most of the paint had worn off and vines had grown over the canoe, hiding it from plain sight. He noticed that the canoe was worn, except for the letters on the back of the canoe reading *Joyous*, still as bright as ever. He wondered whose this was, and then figured it could have been hers at one time.

He suddenly felt a need to know her story—what was she doing walking into The River? He wanted answers, but decided that pushing right now was not the right move. Buddy got up and made a fire as he sat and waited for Disappointed to come over whenever she was ready.

About twenty minutes after he started the fire, Disappointed got up, slowly trying to fix herself up a bit. Her hair was disheveled, and her clothes were wet and dirty from The River's edge. She looked somewhat withdrawn yet still sat down opposite Buddy by the fire.

Disappointed sheepishly spoke out, "I was dead, or at least I had resigned myself to being dead."

As much as Buddy anticipated what would come out of her mouth next, he decided to let her speak out without any prompting from him.

"How did you get here?" Disappointed asked him, as she looked into the fire.

"Well, um, I was kind of sent here," Buddy replied. "I kind of messed up and saw you on The River's edge looking a little worse for wear about a half hour ago but decided that you might need to be left alone. Then farther down The River, I saw someone I knew, and she showed me that you needed my help. So, I made my way back to you upstream and saw you wading into The River quite deep."

He had added the part about it being upstream hoping it would get him some recognition, but she didn't seem to take notice. After about fifteen minutes of silence, she looked up from the fire and gazed into his eyes, and said, "Why me?"

Buddy didn't think before he spoke—and again felt like the words weren't his—but out came, "You are important."

Well, that was enough for Disappointed, and she again broke into tears. Buddy thought about how much quicker he could get to the bottom of Disappointed's story if he would stop making her cry. But once again, Buddy sat there silently and waited for her to calm herself down.

Disappointed got up, still crying, and glanced into the woods where the partially covered-up canoe was. She stared at it for a few minutes and then looked at Buddy and said, "That used to be mine, ya know."

Buddy looked at the canoe and then looked at Disappointed and said, "I noticed a name written on it, but didn't know whose it was."

"A name?" she asked.

"Yeah, it said *Joyous*."

Buddy knew what was next—crying and silence. But to his surprise, Disappointed's shoulders became unslouched, and her head seemed to lift with confidence as she stared at the canoe and said, "Yes! That's who I am."

He didn't know quite what to say, but looking at her again, he asked, "So, that's what I call you?"

"Yes, sir," she replied with a newfound assurance. "You see, I used to be funny and caring, and it used to be me who made other people feel better about themselves when they were around me. It took me a long time to get there, though. I'm not going to get into it right now because I can't dwell on my past too much. However, I come from a long line of abuse. My father abused everything—from any substance he could get his hands on to all of his family."

She looked right at Buddy and repeated sternly, "*All* of his family." She continued, "My mom was too scared to do anything, and one day he went too far and hit my mother so hard that she died."

Taking a moment to dry her eyes, Disappointed continued, "My sister and my brother were then tossed around from home to home and ended up in some pretty bad places. One day, my sister met someone who shared with her some hope of a Friend who could heal us all of our hurt. We both decided to leave the past behind us and move on to whatever lay ahead. That was my hope, that all the suffering was temporary and did not have to define me.

"I then came on this River and began my journey of hope. I started way upriver and ended up here, when I somehow lost my hope and began remembering all the bad things that had happened to me in the past. I started thinking more and more about what had happened to me, and I felt dirty and unwanted. I could feel the hope rush out of me with every bad thought that crept into my mind.

"I remembered The Friend telling me in the beginning that what I feed will grow. So, if I feed the bad thoughts, they will grow, but if I feed the good thoughts, they will grow. Whichever one grows biggest becomes the driving force in my life. But I failed and let the hopeless thoughts reign. That's when you found me. My sister and I were together for a while, and then our paths separated. I really needed her with me to survive, but The River separated us. I think about her so much and hope she's doing better than I am. She was always so helpful."

Buddy then told her about his experience with Helper, his friend on The River. He thought about all the ways Helper had assisted him, and how she was actually the one who had brought him here. Disappointed stood up and blurted out, "Yes, Joyous is my name."

Just then, both Buddy and Disappointed were startled by someone walking in the woods near them. They both jumped up, and Buddy stood in front of Disappointed, feeling responsible for her at this point. They didn't know who it was, but then Disappointed ran over and hugged the person who Buddy suddenly realized was The Friend. They hugged for a long time, and Disappointed resumed her weeping—but this time it was a different weeping, not so hopeless.

The Friend looked at Buddy and gave him a very re-lieving smile, and Buddy's soul instantly felt nourished. He felt like he was where he was supposed to be and doing what he was meant to do at that moment. The Friend walked over and put His hand out to Buddy's, gave it a warm shake, and motioned for him to sit down next to Joyous.

"So, it looks like we need to work on that a little bit, eh?" The Friend said with a smile, as He looked at Joyous's canoe.

Buddy and Joyous sat by the fire and listened intently to every word that came out of the mouth of their Friend. The words were life, being breathed directly into their souls.

The Friend began talking about thoughts. He said that the apostle Paul was a master at taking *every* thought *captive.* "And he literally meant every thought—captive. He took every thought that entered his mind, analyzed it, and decided whether it was negative or positive, whether it was edifying or whether it was destructive. The destructive thoughts he banished into oblivion, and the healthy thoughts he clung to and dwelled on. If he entertained a negative thought for too long, or noticed that he had given regard to a destructive thought, he rejected it and replaced it with a positive one.

"If you don't replace the bad ones, they grow—and the more you feed them, or dwell on them, the bigger and more destructive they become. Joyous, that's where Buddy found you. The Deceiver had planted all those negative thoughts, and you welcomed them in and fed them. Those thoughts wrecked you to the point that you took on your old identity and forgot the hope that I gave you.

"Buddy, you almost missed this opportunity to serve Joyous. You almost decided that to 'get' (spending time with Helper or feeding your stomach) was more important than 'giving' your time and energy to someone who needed it. Imagine if you hadn't shown up. Where would you be now? Floating down The River or having a nice meal with Helper is where you'd be. Where would Joyous be now?" Buddy felt ashamed and couldn't look Joyous in the eye for the guilt that had risen in him once again. Right then, The Friend said, "Buddy, take that thing you call guilt and make it a conviction, turning it into a positive. Learn from this, and don't ever hesitate to help someone in need. No matter what else is going on in your life. There will always be excuses, but if you turn your back on too many opportunities you will become blind toward them, and you will miss every one. That doesn't sound very majestic, does it?"

Buddy understood what The Friend had done there, and smiled weakly back at him as he sat contemplating all that had just gone down. The Friend then told Buddy and Joyous to write down everything that had just happened—all of it, including what they felt and saw, what they did wrong, and the lessons they learned.

They did this so that they could recall them later and remember what they had come through. The Friend then gave Buddy and Joyous the tools to fix her canoe and get it back in the water.

After a day's work, the canoe was as good as new. They both set off in their canoes and drifted downstream together for a while. They laughed and took in all the sights together. Then Buddy glanced over at Joyous and saw how happy she was, and he thought she was indeed Joyous! That immediately made him think about his own sisters, and he wondered how they were.

As Buddy and Joyous made their way down The River, Buddy noticed Helper on The River's edge. Joyous also caught sight of Helper and jumped out of her canoe in the middle of The River, swam over, and embraced Helper, who had jumped in to meet her halfway. They hugged in the water and made their way back to shore. Buddy thought that this must be some sort of female River bond and decided to continue downstream and give them time together.

Right then, Buddy looked up and saw both Joyous and Helper standing on the edge of the water, bowing toward Buddy with their hands in the prayer position, smiling with smiles so robust that he had never seen anything like it before. With his eyes wet, Buddy turned his focus toward The River ahead and felt more satisfied than ever before in his life, wondering if he would ever meet up with either of them again.

CHAPTER 11

Some Listen and Some Don't

*"The pronouns my and mine seem innocent
enough in print, but their constant and universal
use is significant."*
– A. W. Tozer

Buddy found himself alone again on The River, drifting down, pondering what other adventure might await him today. He felt good about what had happened earlier with Helper and Joyous. He especially hoped to see Helper again on his journey.

As the sun began to set, Buddy saw a group of people on the shore around a fire in what looked like a campsite. It was different from most of the other places along The River. This place seemed more permanent than the others. These were dwellings, and not just the temporary shelters that he was used to seeing and using. As he drifted closer, he noticed that there were quite a few people gathered around, observably having a good time. He decided that he'd rather be alone for a while, and was trying to maneuver toward the opposite side of The River when he felt a thrust forward and looked behind him to see a man in a motorized canoe.

Self-Sufficient began pushing him toward the camp-site, saying, "Hey, dude, come on and join us. Just hang for the night and meet some great people."

Buddy felt like being alone—and honestly, if he had to spend time with anyone, it would be Joyous and Helper, not a bunch of strangers. But somehow Buddy didn't have a choice, since there were now two people dragging his canoe up onto the shore. He looked up at them and said, "Uh, thank you?"

One of the guys said, "No worries, mate—glad to see a new face."

Then they presented Buddy to the group and said, "Hey everyone, this is... um, so what's your name?"

Buddy hesitated for a bit and then said, "My name is, um, Buddy."

Immediately they all looked at him and said, "No way, you're Buddy? That's crazy—someone was just talking about you earlier today."

Buddy thought that was super strange and waited for the punch line of the joke. But then a girl chimed in and said, "Yeah, someone said that The Deceiver was looking to find you."

Buddy didn't know what to say. He immediately felt frightened, not so much by what they said, but when he recalled the look The Deceiver had given him when he was struggling to save Disappointed. It was a foul, malicious look that seemed to look deep into his soul.

His new group of friends asked him what he had done to upset The Deceiver, adding that they had never been on the receiving end of a search or threat by The Deceiver. They all seemed to be of the notion that it was better to stay off his radar, but he was powerful and they were all in awe of his capabilities.

Buddy told them the story of Joyous and Helper, and they all listened intently and commented that it was kind of lame that he'd had to paddle upstream to help someone. They said it almost sounded like a consequence, seeming a tad excessive. But then Buddy chimed in and told them that if it wasn't for the hard work or the consequence he experienced to get to Disappointed, he might not have remembered it so clearly.

They seemed to write off what Buddy was saying, and then proceeded to tell him to be careful not to get caught up in truth and consequences. They went on talking about how everyone sees truth differently, and that even though they were all "on" The River, it was natural to have different opinions about what was true. They continued to preach at Buddy that it wasn't about truth and purpose as much as it was about personal development. In their eyes, it was more important to make sure they were getting all they could out of this life and being filled with happiness and good company than to strive to reach some fictitious Waterfall at the end of The River. The Waterfall, in their minds, was hypothetical, not literal. It was a place in the heart that could be wherever they were at the moment. If they had peace, security, good health, and all their needs provided for, that was their Waterfall. There was no room in their theory for an actual Waterfall that led us from this life to the next.

Buddy nodded his head as though he agreed with what they were saying. Once they could tell that he wasn't agreeing with them wholeheartedly, they soon turned their attention to themselves again.

Buddy noticed a smaller group of people sitting closer to the fire and decided to move on, to see if they were any less relative in their outlook on The River. He immediately remembered when The Friend had asked him in the beginning of his journey, "Where are you?" And he wondered if The Friend was asking that of these people right now. They didn't seem to be as interested in what lay ahead on The River as they were in their own thoughts and ideas. The smaller group seemed to be more to Buddy's liking.

Feeling a little discouraged, he lowered his head and left the larger group for The Few by the campfire. They looked up and told Buddy, "Don't worry about them; we're finding that they seem to be in their own little realm over there."

Buddy nodded his head slightly, not sure if that was some sort of trap. But at this point he decided to keep quiet and listen, so he could feel them out as to what they were all about.

One of the guys spoke up and told Buddy that they had overheard him telling the larger group about his recent adventure, and it had hit a certain spot in their hearts. They said they were all just discussing how much they missed that sense of adventure Buddy was describing.

Buddy asked how long they had been there, and three of them responded almost in unison, "Too long."

Then one of the girls spoke up and said, "We were all intrigued at different times with the large group of people on the shore and decided to come and see what was going on. They spoke about peace and security, and how the real meaning of The River is to find happiness. They made the adventure of The River seem obsolete and inconsequential in light of the bigger picture. The whole relativity thing made sense—maybe they were right, and there were no absolutes, and everything was relative. They had all spoken of past times with The Friend and The Guide, so we figured they knew what they were talking about."

Then another one added, "The more you hear them speak, the more you warm up to their theories and find yourself repeating their words as they begin to feel like your own."

Buddy asked them if they had read The Book lately, and they all looked at each other and almost marveled that they had forgotten about The Book and hadn't read it in some time. They also acknowledged that they hadn't written in their own books for quite a while, because there was nothing of significance to write about. Buddy thought how easy it was to fall so far from the truth that The Friend and The Guide had shown him.

He spent the next few hours encouraging these few about getting back to reading and remembering what The Friend had told each of them. They began sharing stories of how good The Friend had been to them and how He had rescued all of them from one thing or another.

After a while one of them looked up at Buddy and said, "Hey, so, if The Deceiver was not after you before, he sure will be on the hunt now."

Buddy didn't know how to take that. He felt good about the time they had all had just now and began to see the reason for his coming to this shore, but he also thought that the advice of The Many, about keeping off The Deceiver's radar, seemed pretty solid.

He then heard a voice in his head that sounded like The Guide that said in a very direct tone, "If you're not on The Deceiver's radar, you're not a threat!"

Buddy knew immediately that he was significant, that The Deceiver being after him was a good thing, and that at the end of the day, The Friend and The Guide were more powerful than The Deceiver.

Feeling especially rejuvenated by his recent time with The Few, he felt as though he should talk again to the larger group. He walked up and, fresh off his success with The Few, began to address The Many about how the adventure of The River and their time with The Friend was missing in their lives. Feeling bolder, he motioned to The River and said that their theories were actually in direct opposition to the things The Friend had taught them. Expecting to reap the same results from The Many as with The Few, Buddy waited quietly for the recognition of the group, only to hear a roar of laughter from the crowd.

One of them spoke up. "Okay, Buddy, how long have you been around The River? Five minutes? Exactly—come find us when you reach that mythical Waterfall!" They all resumed their chuckling, and Buddy felt like he had just wasted his breath.

He walked back to the campfire for some last words with The Few, when one of them said, "Dude, we were just reading this, and I think it's for you: 'Do not reprove a scoffer, or he will hate you; reprove a wise man, and he will love you. Give instruction to a wise man, and he will be still wiser; teach a righteous man, and he will increase in learning. The fear of The Friend is the beginning of wisdom, and the knowledge of the Holy One is insight."[19] Keep on your track, Buddy; don't get caught up in the ones who reject you. Remember all the good you've done so far and keep moving forward."

The Few got up from the campfire. Each of them hugged Buddy, removed the growth from their canoes, and set off again onto The River, spreading out in several different directions.

* * *

It was getting dark, and as Buddy stood on the shore, he heard some rapids that were obviously not too far downriver. He thought it might be a good idea to rest up and set off in the morning. But as Buddy watched The Few paddle down The River, he suddenly heard a noise behind him, felt a whack on the back of his head, and fell face first into The River.

When he came to, he was being swept downriver with his canoe, paddle, and all his belongings about twenty yards in front of him. He was coughing up water and trying to breathe as he came to the rapids. The current pulled him under the water and then slammed him into a large rock in the middle of The River. As he

---

19 Proverbs 9:8-10 ESV (replaced God with Friend)

was being pinned against the rock, he looked back at the shoreline and saw a vague figure on the shore who was most definitely The Deceiver.

The Deceiver looked in his direction and smiled as he turned his back and walked toward The Many. Buddy didn't have time to dwell on why this had been allowed to happen to him, or whether he deserved it or not. He suddenly remembered a verse from The Book that he had memorized: "Even though I walk through the valley of the shadow of death, I will fear no evil, for you are with me; your rod and your staff, they comfort me."[20]

He thought that His Words were near, and so his Friend was, too. He immediately knew that he could overcome this attack and that he was not dying today. Immediately, he was dragged under again and tossed along The River's bottom for what seemed like miles. He had no more strength to fight and was totally exhausted. He let go and blacked out.

* * *

Buddy woke up on The River's edge in the dark and noticed that his canoe was overturned on the shore next to him. He got up and instantly dropped back down to his knees, for he was lightheaded and weak. He crawled over to his canoe and pulled it further up to the shore and brought his belongings closer to where

20 Psalm 23:4 ESV

he lay on the shore, thanking The Friend that he was still alive and had survived the attack. As he lay on the ground, not able to muster the strength to get up, he noticed that the sky was full of stars and he marveled at them, and fell asleep dirty, soaked, exhausted, and badly bruised.

CHAPTER 12

But Joy Comes in the Morning

"Some days are all good, and some days are all God."
– Me

As Buddy woke up, he heard the crackle of a fire and felt the sun on his face. He tried to look over to see who had made the fire, but his neck hurt so badly that he couldn't move. Then he heard a familiar voice and almost had a hard time placing it.

Joy swept over him as he mustered the strength to look over and saw that his sisters Cheerful, Smart, and Funny were there, drying his stuff and making him some food. Cheerful ran over and leaped on Buddy like a fat sack of potatoes. Buddy let out a huge groan and felt like he was going to throw up!

Then Funny yelled over, "Pansy!"

Buddy chuckled, but it hurt so badly to laugh. He looked down and Cheerful was lying on him, hugging him—no matter how much pain he was in, he was so overwhelmed that they were here that he forgot the pain. He suddenly remembered what had happened to him last night and was so grateful that those three were here with him. He had a sense that he should cherish this time as if he would never see them again.

He was ecstatic to be alive and felt even more fortunate to be with them. All three helped Buddy over to the fire, and Smart took a page out of Funny's book and said with a grin, "Hey Buddy, lookin' good."

Buddy figured he looked fairly used up at this point—probably not half as bad as he felt, though. He looked over at the three of them and still could not believe that he was here now, with them. He could die here and be content with this whole journey. He asked hesitantly, not wanting to offend them, "What are you guys doing here?"

They all looked at each other and smiled.

"Well," Cheerful said, "We would follow you anywhere, and once you left for this journey and we found out about it, we knew we had to come and find out what this was. We met The Friend by The River, and He said it needed to be a decision that each of us made for ourselves and not for you. So, we stayed there for a few days as He shared all about this journey and the Decision. He touched all of our hearts so that we saw no other option but to come down The River.

"He told us that at some point He would separate us so that we could be stronger in our own walk with Him, but for now we were granted the gift of traveling together. We always hoped, but never quite knew if we would ever see you here. Until last night. I was awakened by a Voice that said someone needed us. We packed up our stuff and went down The River, not knowing what was in store but knowing that someone was in need. We were so excited at the prospect of helping that we jumped in our canoes and got going."

Buddy was amazed with each word that came out of Cheerful's mouth. Each word was like a ray of joy that touched his heart. To see them all here with him now, on this same journey, was almost more than he could handle emotionally. The other two chimed in as they relayed to him all they had encountered and heard about him on The River.

They talked all day and into the night. This carried on for four days straight, all of them falling asleep by the fire snuggled close together, enjoying every second.

As the sun shone on them the morning of the fifth day, they all awoke to the feeling of gratefulness to be there together. They each felt like it might be the last time, but wouldn't speak it for fear that it would become official. While they were all cleaning up from a quiet breakfast, Cheerful spoke up and said, "I have to go."

Just like that—not real emotional, just a matter of fact. They could all tell that she was being sensitive to them, but that she obviously had heard a call to go. She explained that she had clearly heard the voice of The Guide in her head, telling her that she was about to have an adventure apart from the others for now.

Buddy grew so gloomy in his heart that he couldn't even mutter a word. Then Cheerful came right over to him, laid her head on his shoulder, and said, "It has to be, Bro. As much as I wish it would be a journey with you, for now, it's not. I must learn some things on my own and as scary as that is, it's where I need to be."

As she consoled Buddy and the others, they all noticed that she had already packed her stuff and was ready to go. She was not eager to go, but prepared. Buddy suddenly felt fear for her, wondering if she would encounter The Deceiver and how she would handle him without his help. But then he remembered how sure she was of The Guide and The Friend, and how they had her "in the palm of their hand," as she had explained last night.

His fear soon turned to excitement, knowing that Cheerful would do wonderful things on The River and beyond. So, as the four of them said their goodbyes, Cheerful set off onto The River. As she vanished in the sunrise, they all sat down on The River's edge and talked about how special Cheerful was and how they hoped to see her again soon.

Smart and Funny wanted to wait for a while—both felt the same as Cheerful but didn't want to drop it all on Buddy at one time. They decided to wait a few more days for Buddy to fully recuperate from his recent beating on The River. The three of them sat around and shared with each other pieces from their own books, and they encouraged each other and laughed so hard at Funny's stories and impressions of some people they had encountered on The River.

It was a wonderful time, but each of them paused from time to time, looking at the empty space next to them, wondering how Cheerful was and if they would get to see her again soon. Smart told Buddy countless stories of how he had impacted them as they grew up, and how that had stayed with them their entire lives and made them who they were. Funny, shaking her head "no" in disagreement, jokingly tried to lighten the mood so she wouldn't cry.

"But really," Funny said, "You have touched so many people here on The River already, and many have touched you. It just goes to show that no one is an island on The River. We all need The Friend, and The Friend uses us to help, assist, and love each other. So, we need people, and we need The Friend. Remember that when you want to be a loner again, ya crazy kid."

Buddy loved the fact that he was here with his sisters talking about this stuff. It seemed like a dream.

The dream ended the next day, when the girls had all their stuff packed up by the time Buddy woke up. He knew what they were going to say, even before they said it. Smart looked at Buddy and said with a smile, "When The Voice calls..."

Buddy nodded in agreement but wanted to keep them here with him for as long as he could. Yet he knew they were right. He felt it himself—that this time had been a gift, and he needed to hold on to them with an open palm, releasing them when the time came, not holding too tightly. Because after all, it was The Friend's River, and He knew best.

Buddy said his goodbyes and watched as they floated downstream, looking back at him, waving and blowing kisses until they disappeared around a corner. Buddy made his way back to the fire, sat down, and began to write about the blessings these past days had been for him. It had been such a surprise, and more than he could have ever asked for.

He thanked The Friend and The Guide for this time and began to get his mind on The River once more, and the adventure that lay ahead.

CHAPTER 13

Let God Be God

"Let God be God. He's pretty good at it."
– Me

When Buddy set out the next day for another escapade on The River, he wondered about Cheerful and hoped that she would be okay. She occupied a tender spot in his heart, and he hoped she would remain safe and as far as possible from The Deceiver. But in his heart, he knew that she was a go-getter and would eventually pose a threat to him. He just hoped that she would be strong enough to withstand whatever he could throw at her.

He bowed his head and began a heartfelt prayer to The Friend and The Guide to help Cheerful on her journey and give her strength. He no longer prayed for safety, because he felt like praying for safety was a trap for the weak—especially since he remembered in what high esteem The Many held safety and security. So, he prayed for strength and wisdom for Cheerful and the rest of his sisters. Then his mind wandered to Helper and Joyous as he mentioned them before The Friend as well. He ended his supplication and felt a sense of achievement that he was thinking about others and supporting them in thought and prayer.

For now, Buddy had to manage his own journey. As he set off once more on the uncertain waters, he felt peace. The sun shining on the water through the trees, the warm breeze, the sound of tiny smacks of water against the canoe, and the gentle rocking back and forth of the boat all worked together to make him feel as though this was another moment he would like to bottle up and save for less peaceful times.

Just as when Buddy had been in the woods resting from his run, enjoying the serene setting, he was suddenly spooked by something—this time, the sound of a motorized canoe. He immediately knew who it was. It was Self-Sufficient. He began thinking of all the ways he could try to ignore him or redirect him somewhere else... anywhere else.

He hadn't noticed this before, but when Self-Sufficient stood next to his canoe, Buddy saw that it read Reliant on the side, but that all the letters were dim and barely visible. So apparently, either it was his canoe and his name had changed, or he had stolen it.

He came alongside Buddy, grabbed his canoe, and without asking permission, tied on so they were drifting together. He looked at Buddy and said, "Tired from paddling? You don't have to answer; I'm sure you are. Listen, I would be more than happy to install one of these on your canoe; it saves so much time."

Buddy looked at his motor and then looked back at Self-Sufficient and said, "Well, I think I'm good. Not having a motor allows me to work for what I need to work for, and if I had a motor, I would go anywhere I wanted all the time—and knowing me, I would probably listen to The Guide that much less."

"Well, well, a know-it-all, eh? I'll have you know that I am much more productive with this motor. I can go upstream or downstream, and I can navigate to anywhere I please, making me much more valuable to The Friend and his missions, should I choose that direction. I can help anyone at any time."

Buddy nodding in half-hearted agreement and responded by saying, "Oh, so you help a lot of people?"

"Well, I will once I am fully equipped and have everything I need on this canoe. I mean, I need a tow strap, maybe some longer ropes, a first aid kit, and lots of extra food and water. Once I accumulate all those things, I am going to do amazing things for people. But also, right now, I travel around to different gatherings of many people like the one I met you at, and I tell them all the latest trends and theories from other groups of

The Many. We then take the best and brightest theories from each group and strive for those.

"So, who would do that for these people if I didn't have a motor to propel me wherever I wanted to go? Plus, I don't have to ask The Guide or The Friend for every little thing. I can just do it on my own. And that, my friend, makes me very Self-Sufficient. I used to rely on everything The Guide told me, or what I thought He told me, but that got old. I spend much less time listening now and a lot more time doing; that, too, makes me more productive than ever before."

Buddy again looked at the motor, thinking that the thing that Self-Sufficient thought was an advantage was really a hindrance, stopping him from doing what The Friend wanted him to.

Buddy replied, "Well, what if the point of all of this is to listen patiently for The Guide and The Friend to speak to us, to let us know exactly what we're supposed to do and when we are supposed to do it? And why not help a little, and then work up to helping much? Helping with the little things is important, because they are often the things that mean the most to people. It doesn't have to always be a grand gesture."

If Self-Sufficient wasn't upset with Buddy before, he sure was now. He looked at him, and ignoring his last comment, said, "Well, have a nice day rowing and listening, while I go and do!"

With that, Self-Sufficient unlatched their canoes and set off upstream. Buddy was sad for Self-Sufficient, but kind of glad to see him go at the same time.

As Self-Sufficient headed upstream, he looked back at Buddy and said, "By the way, from here on out The River is easy and takes little effort—so you probably won't need a motor anyway, because you're close to the base of the Waterfall."

Buddy wasn't sure how to take that, but thought that he could use some easy paddling and was psyched that The River was coming to an end. He thought it was really quite easy, all in all. He let go a bit in his mind, relishing the fact that he had passed most of the hard parts of The River, the end was in sight, and maybe he would see the people he missed sooner than he had thought.

He paddled downriver for what seemed like hours and hours, and then he caught sight of his two sisters leaving a campsite right beyond some light rapids. He noticed a narrow path to the left, which seemed calm, and then a broad way to the right, which was where his sisters were getting into their canoes.

He yelled out to them, but they couldn't hear him over the sound of the rapids. He motioned with his hands and waved like a lunatic, yelling for them, but they still didn't hear him. He decided to paddle as hard as he could and get down to them quickly, before they were out of sight, but right then he noticed The Guide next to a bright red flowering bush on The River's edge to the left, motioning for Buddy to paddle to the left, down the narrow path, opposite where his sisters were entering the water.

The red bush was the thing that stuck out to Buddy and caught his attention so that he then noticed The Guide. Buddy pointed to indicate where his sisters were, and The Guide pointed back at Buddy to say that he needed to go in the direction He was pointing. Buddy pretended that he was distracted by the light rapids and lost sight of The Guide, and he went in the direction of his sisters, paddling as fast as he could, fixing his eyes on his sisters and moving fast.

The Guide was now lower down The River, pointing for Buddy to turn around, come back upriver, and go to the narrow path on the left. Buddy saw Him out of the corner of his eye but didn't make eye contact as he descended quickly toward his sisters. Buddy glanced over once more to where The Guide had been, but He was now nowhere in sight.

As Buddy went through the rapids, he quickly came to where his sisters were boarding their canoes, and he could tell that something was wrong. He continued yelling for them, and they finally recognized that it was him and they waited for him. Buddy pulled up next to them and got out and gave them a big hug.

He saw that they were both upset, and he sat them down and asked them what was wrong. Smart, whose canoe read Courageous—something he had never noticed before—said, "I was paddling downriver, and out came Cheerful from a side channel in a terrible fury, being chased downriver by The Deceiver. We were yelling to her, but she couldn't hear us. They had so much momentum and were going so fast that they went right in front of us, but we couldn't catch up."

"Buddy," Courageous said, "you could not imagine the look on The Deceiver's face—it was like he was going to devour Cheerful."

Smart, now apparently called Courageous, said that a group of people in canoes had come up behind them looking for Cheerful, and they had told the sisters they had just seen Cheerful and The Deceiver. "They went on to tell me that Cheerful had just saved them all from a group of The Many that were holding them captive by subtly confiscating their canoes and trying to convince them, through force, that they would be happier in serving The Deceiver. They said that The Many had made it sound so ideal—eating together, living together in perfect harmony, with no judging and none of the rules and laws that The Friend had put into place, and letting them determine their own truth.

"They convinced everyone that The Guide and The Friend were selfish and only wanted to bring division among people on The River and beyond. They made it sound so perfect. But that's when Cheerful showed up and spoke the truth to everyone, telling them that The Friend had a plan for each of them, that He knew the best possible path for each of them, and that they would never be satisfied in settling for anything less."

Buddy suddenly felt such a great sense of pride in Cheerful and was amazed at how bold she was.

But then Funny chimed in, "Buddy, what you don't know is that The Friend asked Courageous and me to split up and so we did, but I fell into that trap of deception and got so very comfortable there. Everyone thought I was funny, and I made people feel good. I was deceived by the false sense of community and relative truth. I felt good about not having to judge anyone or what anyone did. Once Cheerful saw me, she spoke the truth and showed the willing how to leave—well, the ones who wanted to leave, anyway. Just then The Deceiver came out of nowhere and began chasing Cheerful downriver. The other canoes went after Cheerful to check if she was okay."

Buddy didn't know what to say—his emotions were all over the place: happy and proud of Cheerful, a bit nervous and worried for Funny, and with a sense of deep hatred and a hope for revenge on The Deceiver. Buddy was ready to go after Cheerful, but he could tell that Courageous and Funny were exhausted and worn down by the events that had just taken place. So, Buddy stayed with them there for the night, constantly worrying about Cheerful. But he talked to Courageous and Funny all night about things he thought were relevant to what had just happened. He held them and comforted them.

Early in the morning, they set out to look for Cheerful. Just then, The Guide appeared by their canoes. Buddy suddenly remembered that he had ignored The Guide just yesterday and had disregarded His directions. Buddy suddenly felt nauseous, guilty, and ashamed.

The Guide motioned for Buddy to come over to Him while the girls stayed where they were. The Guide looked at Buddy and said, "Buddy, be careful. The more you ignore Me or convince yourself that I'm not real or that you simply misheard, the easier it becomes to ignore Me and write Me off. Once that happens, you have only yourself to rely on. Does that sound like anyone you know? Self-Sufficient maybe?

"Buddy, you were doing so well, and then you thought you knew better than Me. You thought your sisters needed you. But in reality, they needed Me and their Friend. They went through things that you know nothing about, and yet you attended to them when it was I and The Friend who wanted to. You just taught them that it was you they needed to turn to, and not Me or The Friend. You showed them that their big brother will come to the rescue, and not Me. Was that your intention, Buddy?"

Buddy sheepishly responded, "I am really sorry; I didn't know."

"That's right, Buddy; you didn't know, but yet you ignored My instructions and did what you wanted. Don't do that again, Buddy. I forgive you, but remember that the more you ignore Me, the easier it becomes. The Friend was waiting around the corner to be with your sisters and help them through this. You just put yourself in the place of The Friend. Was that your intention?"

Buddy looked down at the ground, now feeling absolutely discouraged. "I... um..." was all he could muster.

"Buddy, I know you feel bad now. Take that and use it for good. Learn your lesson here and point people to The Friend and not yourself—and Buddy, I am not a good luck charm or One to be ignored. Do not ignore Me."

The Guide gave Buddy a long hug, much longer than Buddy had anticipated, and then Buddy felt like he was almost sinking into a warm blanket. He felt bad but understood now where he had gone wrong. Buddy knew what he had to do. He went over to his sisters and said that they needed to go without him, that there was Someone much more apt to help them than he ever could.

He told them to go and look for The Friend, who was waiting for them. They both hugged Buddy and made their way downriver. The Guide motioned for Buddy to go back to the place where he first saw the red bush by the canal, on the left side of The River. Buddy looked at the rapids and thought how handy a motor would be right about now.

The Guide, knowing exactly what Buddy was thinking, said, "Don't go there, Buddy. Sometimes you have to put in extra effort to make things right. Your actions have consequences."

With that, Buddy got in his canoe and began making his way upriver through the light rapids.

CHAPTER 14

Consequences Do Exist

"There are in nature neither rewards nor punishments—there are consequences."
– Robert G. Ingersoll

Buddy began to break a sweat as he made his way upstream to the narrow path he had ignored the day before. It didn't look all that treacherous, yet the farther he paddled upstream, the more effort it took. It seemed like it was taking more and more effort now to move even a few feet against the current. He felt a hint of irritation creep into his mind. *Wouldn't my time be better spent somewhere else? Isn't there someone who needs my help, or some new lesson I can learn? I mean, for real, what is the point of all of this?*

He thought how easy it would be to just quit going upstream, and fake a muscle strain or let himself go with the flow downriver. But just then a voice came into Buddy's head. *Your actions have consequences.* Buddy remembered that this was the last thing The Guide had said to him. And suddenly, Buddy wasn't so irritated. He felt the shame he had felt when The Guide was talking to him about trying to replace The Friend. He wanted to make sure this would never happen again, and immediately Buddy was glad that this lesson was being etched into his mind.

After Buddy gained this new sense of motivation The River did not get easier, but his willingness to engage and make the most of the situation helped him power through until before he knew it, he was at the narrow path. As he drifted onto the narrow path, Buddy suddenly felt exhausted from the fervor of paddling so hard for so long. He let his canoe drift over to an embankment, where he got out and noticed his pants were soaked from the ride against the rapids. He took them off and laid them on a rock to dry out.

There was a shady patch and a warm breeze, and he thought he would lie down and await further instruction. As he lay under a large tree, he fell fast asleep in a matter of minutes. Buddy peacefully drifted into a dream state and relaxed as his whole body melted into the grassy nook.

But after about an hour, he suddenly felt anxiety for Cheerful. He saw a dark image of The Deceiver speed past in his mind. His heart began to race, and he felt an urge to go and find her and do whatever it took to make sure she was safe. His prayer for strength and wisdom for Cheerful was quickly replaced with a prayer for safety and comfort for her. His mind began racing and he woke himself up, suddenly in a frightful panic. He got up and raced toward his canoe, determined to do whatever it took to find his beloved sister. As Buddy reached for his canoe, he heard a familiar voice coming from The River's edge.

"So, it didn't take long, did it? What's changed from the time we last spoke until now?" The Guide said, reclining on the ground near The River's edge.

"Well, um, Cheerful needs me, and I just have a really bad feeling."

"That's right, Buddy, all you had was a feeling—no word or sign from Me, just an emotion that led you to forget what brought you here—and those lessons you just learned were so quickly discarded. So, now you believe you know better? Better than I do, better than The Friend?"

Buddy kicked a nearby tree in frustration. "Dang it! Why am I so quick to do my own thing? Why do I do that?"

"Well, because that's your nature. That is what you have done your entire life. You did what you thought was best. Before, your life was about you, with a hint of Me here or there. You treated Me like a genie or a good luck charm, but this River is here to teach you to rely on Me. Not on emotions or whims, but on Me, The Friend and Truth. The more attention you pay to Us, the more likely you are to listen and obey. You cannot change everything in an instant, but you can change something today. Change the voice you listen to. Be directed and moved by Me; that, my boy, is success.

"It takes a giant leap, and then a million small steps, but each of those steps is like the rung on a ladder, leading you closer to a solid relationship with Me. That is your goal in all of this. Know Me! Know My voice, and when you hear it, obey. Don't worry about what you do as much as remembering that I am with you always, longing for you to converse and just be with Me.

"Buddy, you're going to get there. It may seem like you're moving backwards at times, but sometimes it's one step back and two steps forward. Give yourself time and continue fighting for what's right, in your mind and around you, every day."

The Guide put His hand on Buddy's shoulder and smiled lovingly as He pointed to the narrow path and spoke enthusiastically to Buddy. "Take care of your mind on this narrow route. It's easy to get off track and wander. Stay focused, and be aware of your surroundings. I will find you later, but for now, stay the course."

Buddy glanced in the direction of the narrow path; he could only see about fifty yards ahead of him, but it looked dense and—well, narrow. He felt a mixture of excitement and remorse. Remorse for the ways in which he had just so badly failed, and excitement for being on the narrow path and overcoming his sins of doubt and self-reliance.

As he headed toward his canoe and began dragging it to The River's edge, he looked back and saw The Guide laughing with a laugh that was so rich. Holding up Buddy's pants, The Guide said jokingly, "You may want these! It might get a bit breezy without them."

Buddy laughed and was amazed at how just a simple laugh made him feel so good. After Buddy put his pants on, he shoved off, ready to travel the narrow path.

CHAPTER 15

Bad Things Happen

"Eat the fruit of sorrow even if it is bitter, because this fruit that you can only eat now has nutrients in it that you can't get any other way."
– John Piper

The narrow path had long twists and turns, but for the most part it was quite nice and relaxing. Then, amid his placid ride, Buddy heard a motor from ahead of him and a scream from down below, which sounded far off. It vaguely sounded like Cheerful. He felt sick to his stomach.

What's the matter? What can I do? Buddy thought. He began to get anxious, and his concern for Cheerful took over all other emotions, but he told himself that he could not leave this path to seek her out. He dropped his paddle in the canoe and dropped to his knees and prayed. He prayed out loud and asked The Guide and

The Friend to go to her rescue and to help him stay the course.

He then felt a tug on his canoe, having forgotten that he had heard the motor just about the same time as the scream. Then he saw Self-Sufficient and immediately said, "Hey, not now, okay? I just heard a scream, and I'm sure it's my sister. The Deceiver was after her, and there is nothing I can do about it because I know I need to be here."

Immediately Self-Sufficient said, "You can't go, but I can. What's her name? I'm on it!"

"Um, hey—thanks. Her name is Cheerful."

Without another word, Self-Sufficient took off, and Buddy only saw the wake that was left by his motorized canoe. Buddy thought that maybe the motor wasn't all bad after all. *I mean, it could save my sister's life!* Buddy thanked God for sending Self-Sufficient and asked forgiveness for judging him.

With a sense of peace, he reengaged The River and paddled, trusting that Self-Sufficient was on the task. *I should really get to know him better when I see him again and not be so quick to think I have all the answers. Maybe he was right; maybe he proved me wrong, and I am a bit of a know-it-all.* With that, Buddy moved on down The River on the narrow path.

After about an hour on this path he came to a clearing, where he could see miles downriver and could even get a glimpse of the base of the Waterfall. As he panned all around, looking for some hope of seeing Cheerful and maybe Self-Sufficient, he noticed down below—not too far away, on a beachy part of The River—someone lying next to their canoe, with several people surrounding them. Then he noticed Self-Sufficient's specially rigged canoe and felt a desperate, sinking feeling in his heart.

He immediately ditched his canoe in a wooded area and ran downhill through the thick brush, passing the spiraling River several times in different spots. He ran down through the woods, and then jumped in and swam frantically through The River. He repeated this several times, until he was close to the spot where they were gathered around the person.

As Buddy got closer, he noticed Self-Sufficient weeping on the edge of The River by himself, his canoe overturned in the water, stuck on a rock with the motor torn off. Then he saw Funny and Courageous holding Cheerful in their laps. She lay draped across her sisters, void of any movement. His sisters just sat there, weeping and holding her tight. Buddy didn't know what to think. He was bleeding and scarred from his mix of tumbling and almost drowning to get down the mountain.

His sisters saw him and held their arms out, motioning to him to come and sit with them. Buddy couldn't move; he was angry at The Friend for letting this happen and didn't know how to express himself. He was filled with rage, and then he spotted Self-Sufficient. In a frenzy he ran over to him, picked him up, and began punching him repeatedly in the face. He couldn't stop. Then before he knew it, his sisters both had come over and were pulling with all their strength to get him off. "What are you doing? Have you lost your mind?" Funny said with a tone of disapproval. "What's wrong with you?"

"He killed her, didn't he? He can never do anything right—always doing his own thing," Buddy said piously.

"No, Buddy—he tried to save her, but it was too late."

"Oh, your precious motor wasn't enough this time? Shocker. Maybe trust in something other than yourself for once. How does it feel to know your life is a waste?"

Self-Sufficient now lay on the ground looking up at the sky, still weeping, but now holding his face and trying to contain his pain.

Courageous looked at Buddy. "You're lucky that Cheerful wasn't here to see that."

Buddy just fell to the ground and looked at Cheerful's peaceful, innocent face. He began to weep uncontrollably, and his sisters both hugged him and held him until he ceased crying.

"How?" is all that Buddy could muster.

Courageous looked at Buddy and began to tell him what they saw as they arrived on the scene. "Cheerful had deflected an attempt by The Deceiver to thwart her mission to help as many people as possible. He tried to scare her into fleeing and cowering from his presence. But she was actually leading The Deceiver away from those she thought were frail and not able to fight him. We thought she was fleeing for her own safety, but she was acting in a way to save others.

"That's when we saw you. She didn't need our help. If anything, she was showing us how to be brave and fight for other people's well-being. She deceived The Deceiver, and he was angry. He then set his sights on another group of young Seekers who were being led down a path that led to a steep waterfall that no one could survive. Someone who witnessed the whole thing told us what happened. As Cheerful had made her way down The River, frantically trying to save as many as she could, she came upon a group she had seen several days before. She noticed that they were easily led astray and were very new to The River. She saw Helper and spent some time with her, and told her that she had prayed that she would have an opportunity to help them. I guess she and Helper had a good time together. She was just here, and she left after she prayed with us and said her goodbyes to Cheerful. She was called somewhere else, I guess. She filled us in on some of it. But the ones she saved—"

Buddy interrupted, "The ones she saved?"

"Yes—those over there, lying on the other side of the shore. She saved all of those people."

Buddy looked, and there were at least twenty people across The River, crying and talking with The Guide. Intrigued, Buddy looked back at Courageous, motioning to her to finish the story.

"I was told it like this: There were these twenty or so people being targeted by The Deceiver, and Cheerful, wanting to help and encourage them, felt led to follow them and see what she could do. The group was being led by The Deceiver down The River toward the impassable waterfall. They seemed eager to go, since The Deceiver had told them that it was a shortcut to the base of the Waterfall. Cheerful paddled up next to them and began a discourse with the group in the presence of The Deceiver.

"'Hey guys, nice day. By the way, who told you that this was a good path to take? Don't you know that this guy,' pointing to The Deceiver, 'only cares about you *not* getting to your destination?' Cheerful asked them.

"One from the group answered, 'But the base of the Waterfall is our destination.'

"The Deceiver chimed in, 'I am only leading them to where they were told to go. See, you have me all wrong; I can be a great help if people only listen to me.'

"'He has a point, don't you think? I mean, we want to get to the base of Waterfall, no?' another person said.

"Cheerful paddled in front of the group and positioned herself between the group and The Deceiver so that everyone could hear her. 'Well, actually, who told you that the base of the Waterfall was your destination? Were you not told in the beginning that the point of this journey is the journey itself, and who the journey is with? Not any one destination? Don't be too quick to run to wise-sounding and flattering words. This guy is only here to deceive you and make you overlook the real point of all of this. Didn't The Guide make it clear that there are no shortcuts, and that the most important thing is the process? Your desired destination can be achieved by simply knowing The Guide and The Friend and heeding their voices. That is the destination.'

"They had heard that before, but coming from one so young and so sure, it spoke so deeply to them that they all stopped paddling and asked Cheerful what to do next.

"'Wait for The Guide. He wants to speak with you about today and about what you can learn from all of this deception. He wanted me to ask you to wait at The River's edge for Him to come, no matter what happens and no matter what you see or are told.'

"As the group made their way to the shore, Cheerful noticed that The Deceiver was leaving, but one person in the group was still following him. She saw the group to the shore and then raced to the one who continued with The Deceiver. She went all the way to the Waterfall, and they both fell from the top. We saw it all happen in slow motion, and we frantically looked for them, but the one who had followed The Deceiver surfaced first and could be seen throwing up water at the base of the Waterfall. Then we finally found Cheerful like this on The River's edge."

Just as they were finished telling what had transpired, The Friend came by and gently took Cheerful from them and waded into the water in the direction of The Waterfall. No words were spoken, but soon, Cheerful and The Friend vanished into the base of The Waterfall. A second before they vanished, as the rest of the group began looking away and staring at each other, Buddy saw Cheerful's arms wrap around her Friend's neck. Buddy thought he must have been seeing things.

There were so many pieces to put together. Self-Sufficient was devastated. Funny and Courageous were tending to him, but they were gutted on the inside that their sister was gone. And Helper could be seen watching everything happen from up on top of the Waterfall.

Courageous felt terrible about the loss of her sister and the sorrow it had caused the others. But she had never seen such an act of selflessness and compassion for others. Courageous sat up and asked the others if they wanted to pray. No one looked up. She then began to relay a message The Friend had told her before she had begun her journey.

She talked about loss, and how it affected people differently. She was told that loss is a part of The River, a part of life everywhere. How we deal with loss also determines our path for the rest of our lives. People either get angry and bitter, or they accept the loss as a natural part of life and learn to rely on The Friend more because of it. That's not saying that people need to ignore loss or pretend it doesn't hurt, but to remember that there is One who has also suffered loss and knows how to heal our hurt. That if we reach out to Him, He will heal us.

Courageous then said that they should all pray and ask The Friend for help. No one responded. As the minutes turned into hours, each person began to get up and leave in separate directions. Funny trotted away as if she were trying to get away from something. Buddy tried to dodge Self-Sufficient's glance, pretending that he forgot he was there, but as their eyes met, Self-Sufficient looked for some consolation in Buddy's eyes. He found none.

Self-Sufficient went, downtrodden, into the woods as Buddy began to rage that the kindest, most generous and caring person on The River was now gone. His anger drove him, too, into the woods. With every step, Buddy got more and more heated at Self-Sufficient, The River, The Guide, and The Friend for not saving the only one worthy of being saved. As everyone scattered in different directions, Helper, from the top of the Waterfall, got on her knees and prayed for them all and thanked The Friend for being there with her.

CHAPTER 16

Down the Valley

"Talk to yourself more than you listen to yourself."
– Martyn Lloyd Jones, *Spiritual Depression*

Buddy found himself wanting to be alone. Not just alone, but so far away from everyone that he went out of his way to find the most solitary spot he could. He only thought of his sorrow, anger, and sense of injustice over what had happened to Cheerful. Buddy began thinking about The Guide and The Friend. *That's what you get for helping others, I guess, Buddy thought. Why would I trust Them, when They can't even look out for those who love Them? Do They really love those people on The River? Do They really control anything?* As Buddy got deeper and deeper into his angry thoughts about The Friend, he couldn't see anything but doubt, rage, and sadness.

Helper got up off her knees and sat quietly on the edge of the Waterfall. She sat silent as she listened for the voice of The Guide. Although she was heartbroken at what she had just seen transpire down below, she knew that The Friend was the only one who would have the answers. She waited in peace, knowing that the only One with the answers would speak in His own time. The silence became sprinkled with the sounds of a multitude of different birds, distributing their own unique sounds into the air. Some were subtle, some profound; some came in small bursts, some lasted for what seemed like minutes. It was such a peaceful arrangement that seemed just for her.

As she listened to the orchestra of birds, she began to doze off into a light slumber. As she fell into a deep sleep and began to dream, Helper saw a raccoon, ferocious and larger than any she had ever seen, creep slowly into a chicken coop filled with baby chicks. The fencing was sturdy all around, making entry by unwanted predators almost impossible. Helper became fearful of what was about to take place and felt herself becoming increasingly anxious. In an instant, the raccoon began racing toward the chicks, causing the chicks to scatter and leave the safety of the coop.

The chicks, in fear, all found a way to get underneath the fence and spread in all different directions. She opened her eyes and heard a Voice saying, "Tend to the chicks." Helper knew immediately what she needed to do. She got up, thanked The Friend and The Guide, and set off to help mend some broken hearts.

* * *

Buddy walked upriver to try to find his canoe and then thought, *Why do I even need that canoe? I can find one if I find one, but if not, I can make camp somewhere and think about what I'm going to do.*

Buddy felt his thighs get heavy from the climb up the hill. He was exhausted and tired—emotionally, and now physically. As he walked a little more, he saw one of the old canoe sites that lay on the edge of The River. It was large and looked like it had been used at one time for launching canoes. A number of canoes had been overgrown with reeds, bushes, and vines. They were weathered, but each was unique.

I'll use them for firewood, Buddy thought. He thought that maybe if he burned them, he'd save others from the heartache he felt. Buddy's mind was so tangled in doubt and hurt that he no longer thought about The Friend, or where he should be, or what he should be doing.

Buddy grabbed some of the canoes and concocted a shelter using them. He gathered some wood, found some berries, and set up his camp for the foreseeable future. In his quietness and sorrow, Buddy began thinking about Cheerful. He grew even more sad and started softly crying once more.

He got up and found a canoe that looked like it was made from a white birch tree. It was bright white with light brown strands running all over it. Even though it was weathered, it was beautiful. Buddy broke that up and decided to make a little shrine to Cheerful by The River's edge. He put his locket from her on it, etched her name, and wrote: *To the one who deserved the world.*

Buddy stood back and admired what he had built. He thought, Even if she's not valued by The Friend and The Guide, I will honor her. With that, Buddy lay under the shelter he had made and fell asleep while staring at the shrine to Cheerful.

He awoke to the sun shining and the sound of someone coming to The River's edge through a path in the woods. It was faint, but became louder and louder. It sounded like someone was crying softly. To Buddy's surprise, Sorrowful came to the edge of The River where Buddy had set up camp. She broke through the woods and came right over to him. "I need a break. I just need a few minutes to gather my thoughts and rest," said Sorrowful. She was younger than Buddy, and beautiful. She didn't seem to take much notice of him but seemed to speak to him out of courtesy, since he had been there first. She went over and lay under the shrine, obviously not noticing what it was, but seemed to fall right to sleep. Buddy was bothered that she lay by the shrine but intrigued that she was there. He wanted to be alone, but this was okay, since it took his mind off his sorrow.

* * *

He woke up to the sounds of the rapids in The River, and as he opened his eyes, he saw Sorrowful staring at him. She quickly blurted out, "So, is this your place?"

"Well, um, I guess it is," Buddy said without confidence. "I came here to get away from things for a while."

"Man, that sounds good," Sorrowful said with a deep sigh. "It's been a hard road, and I just need to think about something else for a while."

Buddy understood what she was saying but was fascinated with what her story might be. *Why is she here? What's her story?* She just jumped right in, telling Buddy why she was there looking for refuge.

"I've had enough of people using me. I don't know you, but I feel like you're probably one of the good guys. From as early as I can remember I've been used by people for whatever they wanted, whenever they wanted. I don't want to be there—I want to be somewhere far away, somewhere I don't know anyone. Somewhere I can start fresh."

Buddy thought he should mention The Friend to Sorrowful, but then thought that he wasn't even sure anymore how good of a Friend He was. So, he ignored his instinct and began telling Sorrowful what he would have told Cheerful if she was there in front of him. He began with simple, generic things about being unique, one of a kind. Then he took what he knew about her so far and used that too.

"It took a lot of courage to stop here and come meet me. I can tell you're adventurous, independent, and one of the prettiest people I've ever seen." Buddy immediately felt awkward when those words came out of his mouth.

Sorrowful seemed just as awkward when she heard the words. But she also felt a sense of empowerment and liberation with every word Buddy spoke to her. As tears began to well up in her eyes, she began to feel alive—and for the first time in a long time, she felt important.

Buddy could tell he was reaching her soul with his words. He ran out of things to say but didn't want her to know, so he nonchalantly stood up and said, "You seem tired and probably need some time alone and some rest. Make yourself at home, and I'll go find some food."

Sorrowful slept for hours. Buddy thought she had probably had a rough go of it for quite a while and just needed some encouragement and affirmation. That had always seemed to work with Cheerful.

As Sorrowful woke up, she felt an instant connection to Buddy. He seemed so wise, so thoughtful. From then on, every word he spoke seemed like life and truth. He filled a void in her that had seemed empty for so long. It felt nice to be encouraged. Sorrowful wanted to do something for Buddy; she wanted to make him feel the same way he made her feel. She noticed that Buddy had gathered some food and stopped by the shrine, looking sadly into the sky as he touched the locket.

Buddy suddenly looked at Sorrowful and knew his purpose. He was good at encouraging people, at making people feel special. After all, look at Sorrowful—she seemed a lot better than when she first got here. The shrine would serve as a beacon to those who were hurt.

They can come here, and I will make sure that they are taken care of, that they are encouraged and made to feel special. This was Buddy's purpose, his way to live as a tribute to Cheerful. As he was having this epiphany, he noticed Sorrowful talking to some people on The River's edge about what that shrine was and what they were doing there. He overheard her talking about how he had helped her and spoken life into her soul. She hugged them and walked them over to Buddy.

Buddy sat them down and began listening to them, hearing what they were saying and trying to figure out what they needed, or needed to hear. He began to speak encouraging words to them, talking about how simple our needs are and how freely we can live in harmony by simply encouraging each other.

* * *

As the hours turned into days and the days into weeks, more and more people came to be around The Many Encouragers, as people began to call them. Soon there were a few dozen people living together and finding their own truth about life, as they retreated from The River. Their canoes were shoved into the woods or used to make tables, shelters, and other useful things.

Buddy finally felt good—well, better than he had in a while. He often thought about Cheerful, and how proud she would have been of him if he could only see him now.

One day, as Buddy was greeting new people, he noticed that a new group was being led by someone right to his edge of The River. This person seemed familiar, but Buddy couldn't place him in his mind. As he welcomed them to the sanctuary Buddy had created, he looked across The River and saw The Guide. That shook Buddy to the core.

Because of how deeply devastated and sad his recent thoughts had been, and because he felt so lost, The Guide seemed so distant to him mentally. He had not even thought about Him through any of this. He tried to pretend he couldn't see Him, but something made him look at Him again. When he looked back at The Guide, he noticed that Self-Sufficient was the one leading people to the shore. He hadn't thought about him in quite some time, either.

First, Buddy thought angry thoughts, but then he thought that he too could probably use some encouragement. As Buddy went over to try to get his attention, he noticed The Guide, who was pointing at another figure flowing upstream with a huge smile on his face, also pointing people to Buddy's sanctuary. Yet another person he had not seen or thought of in a while—The Deceiver.

The Guide was motioning to show Buddy that The Deceiver seemed pleased with what Buddy was doing; that he somehow approved. That immediately made Buddy feel sick, and he went white. When Buddy looked back, The Guide was gone, and some of the people there gathered around Buddy and helped him sit down, because it looked like he was about to faint.

CHAPTER 17

Enough

"It was pride that changed angels into devils; it is humility that makes men as angels."
– St. Augustine

Helper and Courageous were on a quest. They wanted to help mend the hearts of those who were hurt by what had happened to Cheerful. With the help of The Friend and The Guide, they set out to help heal those who had been hurt. As soon as they entered the woods they came across Funny, who was sitting by The River's edge, throwing rocks into The River. She seemed almost bored, like she didn't know what to do with herself. She had always found comfort in making people laugh, in, well—being Funny. She could always lighten a mood or change an uncomfortable situation. She was lost because she couldn't find the strength or mental capacity to change what had happened through being funny.

She was angry at Buddy for beating Self-Sufficient, devastated over losing Cheerful, and she hurt deeply. As Helper sat down, she put her arm around Funny and didn't say a word. Funny let her head rest on Helper's shoulder, closed her eyes, and began to weep softly. As Funny started to feel a little embarrassed for being so weak, Courageous sat down on the other side of her and put her hand on her thigh and sat in silence with them both.

After a long time of quiet, Funny said, "I knew I should have prayed with you, Courageous. I felt something deep in my soul tell me to pray. But then another voice came into my head, telling me that if I couldn't make people laugh, what good was I? I immediately felt useless, angry, and helpless, so I fled. I should have prayed—I should have listened to that Voice."

As soon as she stopped talking, Helper said, "Hey, you are Enough."

"What?" Funny replied.

"You are Enough. The Friend told me that your name is certainly Enough. Because you know Him, because you are one of His own, you are Enough. Not because you're funny, which you are. But because of who He has made you. You have so much to offer. Stop striving to compete, never being satisfied and always needing to be the fixer of situations. You, Funny, are Enough."

"Wow," was all that Courageous could muster, as she sat in awe of what Helper had said.

They all sat there for the next little while, staring at The River. Courageous began praying out loud for them, for Cheerful, for Self-Sufficient, and mostly for Buddy. They all became immediately concerned for Buddy.

"I need to tell you guys something," Helper said sheepishly. "I spent a bunch of time on The River with Cheerful. I know you guys know her so much better than I do, but Cheerful was special. She had a special relationship with The Guide and The Friend also. She knew she would leave The River early, or earlier than would seem appropriate. She also knew that Buddy had some tough lessons ahead." She paused, not knowing how to proceed. But she continued, "She knew that Buddy would react the way he did that day by The River's edge when she passed on. She told me that we were to help Buddy, but that there would be some time when we could do nothing. She said not to worry, because he would learn some precious lessons and then be restored, greater than he could ever imagine."

"We need to pray for guidance here," said Enough.

They prayed together, seeking wisdom, grace, and the endurance to move forward, thanking The Friend for Cheerful as well.

* * *

Buddy felt dizzy; he had so many thoughts running through his head. *How far have I strayed from when I first started on this River? How is what I am doing here any different from what I was doing before I came to The River? It all happened so fast. What is my purpose here?*

As these thoughts raced through his head, he slowly heard the voices of those around him getting louder and louder and going from background noise to the forefront, coming more and more into focus. They were asking Buddy if he was okay. He said he was, but he just needed some time.

Buddy left them and went over to the shrine, lay down, and began to think about what his end game was here. He felt hopeless; he had lost his favorite person in the world, and he had returned to his old ways of doing as he saw fit.

Sorrowful gave Buddy some time to himself but then came over to him. She sat down in front of him, placed one hand on either shoulder, and said, "Buddy, what happened by The River? You seemed frightened and miserable all at once. Everyone is asking what's wrong with you, and why you're not talking to anyone. These people look up to you and want to help you if you need it."

Buddy felt even worse that he had these people now looking to him for consolation and comfort. *If they only knew,* he thought, *how incapable I am, they would never look to me for anything.*

He got up and told everyone that he needed to be alone for a while, and that he was leaving but would be back when he had sorted some things out. He left Sorrowful in charge, although she didn't look like she was impressed with the responsibility or with Buddy leaving. She motioned for everyone to come with her and to leave Buddy alone.

"I guess he needs some time. Let's get some food and get ready for dinner," Sorrowful said, obviously hurt.

Buddy began walking along The River's edge, not headed anywhere in particular, but just walking. He came to an area that looked familiar and surprisingly found his canoe in the woods. It was set up with all his stuff, sitting in the woods as if someone had set it aside for him.

He removed the brush, cleared it off, and set it in The River. As he got in and started downriver, he saw Self-Sufficient leading more people to the site. He stared at Buddy, shrugged his shoulders and mouthed, "Where are you going?"

Buddy made a noncommittal grin and kept paddling downriver.

He then started floating, with his paddle in the boat, out of the water. He wanted to float—not work, just float. He lay down in the canoe and thought back to the first time he had set off on The River, how he had expected something special and then was launched out of his canoe. He remembered how frustrated that had made him feel, but then he remembered how he had met Helper because of that. This made him smile.

As Buddy drifted downriver, he eventually found himself on an offshoot of the main River, a side channel of water that led away from The River but was still part of the central source. It was narrow and serene. It had winding bends and sandy shorelines. Buddy noticed an opening in The River and a beach surrounded by palm trees. He beached his canoe and got out and scouted out the site.

It looked like people had been here not too long ago. There were hammocks, leftover food, and a primitive but clean shelter. Buddy thought that people might live here and that they would probably be back, but he was tired and mentally exhausted and decided to stay for a while. As he took his bag out of the canoe, The Book dropped out and opened to a page that was highlighted. He picked it up and read, "Now when The Friend heard this, He withdrew from there in a boat to a desolate place by himself."[21]

Buddy took The Book and sat down on The River's edge. He read a little before and after that verse and saw that it was about The Friend losing someone He

---

21 Matthew 14:13 ESV (replaced Jesus with The Friend)

loved dearly, and going to a solitary place to deal with it. Buddy knew what that verse was for. In an instant he knew that The Friend had withdrawn and probably wept, and he sought the correct response to the injustice, grief, and devastation of losing his sister. How much sorrow and false sense of good would Buddy have circumvented had he taken this approach right away.

He put down The Book and prayed out loud. "Friend, Guide, I am so weak. I'm no good without You. I can't seem to get out of my own way and live on The River like I should. I cause myself and other people heartache and pain. I don't know how to do this, but I know You do. Help me, forgive me, and allow me to do better, make things right, and get to know You more, no matter what circumstance I find myself in." With that, he lay down, closed his eyes, and felt a peace come over him, and he rested.

When Buddy woke up, it was dark. He felt like he had slept for days. He felt strong, energized, and ready for an adventure. As he was standing up, he saw The Book lying next to the hammock he had borrowed. He felt like he was supposed to spend some time reading, praying, and just being in the presence of The Friend and The Guide, even if just in thought. Buddy lay on the hammock and began reading.

"Are there any among the false gods of the nations that can bring rain? Or can the heavens give showers? Are you not He, O Lord our God? We set our hope on you, for you do all these things."[22]

Buddy started contemplating this passage and read that there was another linking passage somewhere else in The Book, so he turned to that page and read, "I rejoiced in The Friend greatly that now at length you have revived your concern for me. You were indeed concerned for me, but you had no opportunity. Not that I am speaking of being in need, for I have learned in whatever situation I am to be content. I know how to be brought low, and I know how to abound. In any and every circumstance, I have learned the secret of facing plenty and hunger, abundance and need. I can do all things through Him who strengthens me."[23]

Buddy read these and thought, *Through* Him *who strengthens me, and in* Him *I hope. It's all about* Him. *It's also about* Him *being with me and making me able to succeed and to remain faithful in good times, bad times, times I feel strong, and times I feel weak. It's not about me and what makes me happy, what makes me comfortable or secure. Being good is not good enough. Being friendly, patient, or well-intentioned is not enough. Apart from* Him, *there is nothing. But I can do all things through* Him.

---

22 Jeremiah 14:22 ESV
23 Philippians 4:10-13 ESV (replaced Lord with Friend)

He knew this was something very significant, something of an epiphany. He put The Book down and thought about what this would mean for him, and why it was true. He saw how opposed to The Friend his little shrine community was. He was once again becoming a savior to people only God could heal. He sat in silence, contemplating more. He felt ashamed; he felt unworthy of being known by The Friend, because he kept disappointing Him. What would it take to become a friend to The Friend? Was he even worthy to call Him Friend?

As Buddy was thinking on all these things, he felt a presence near him, as if something were watching him. He got instantly nervous. Then, as he was peering into the woods, he saw a shadowy figure coming toward him. Buddy began to clench his fist and get ready for a fight.

Then, before he could stand up, he heard, "Yeah, please don't hit me. I'm still healing from the last time." Self-Sufficient was half joking, half serious. Buddy felt in his heart that he would somehow need to make amends for what he had done wrong, and that now was his opportunity.

Buddy knew that Self-Sufficient was trying to make amends with him by leading people to his little place by The River. He could feel that Self-Sufficient was trying to please Buddy out of remorse for what had gone down. Self-Sufficient was trying to make up for the fact that Buddy was angry with him for not being able to save his sister. Even though Buddy knew it was not Self-Sufficient's fault, it seemed Self-Sufficient did not know that; or that he believed a lie that it was. Buddy asked how he was doing, and Self-Sufficient let him know that he was fine, but he had been sent here by the Encouragers to find him and bring him back. Buddy became embarrassed and fearful of the consequences of leading these people astray in the false hope of Buddy being able to save them.

Self-Sufficient could obviously see the despair on Buddy's face and asked, "So, why are you here? Why do you seem so sad?"

Buddy knew that this was his time to make things right, possibly even to help Self-Sufficient. He kept hearing the word reliant but didn't know what it meant. It stuck in his head and wouldn't depart.

"So, first, I'm sorry," Buddy said. "I'm sorry for taking out my sense of loss and frustration on you. It was not your fault." Buddy saw Self-Sufficient's entire being perk up. So, he felt he should repeat himself. "It was not your fault. You could have done nothing differently that would have changed the outcome that day. I was jealous of your ability to move so freely. I was frustrated with my own situation, and I projected that onto you ever since the first day I met you."

"Oh," was all Self-Sufficient could mutter. But after a few moments he continued,

"I didn't mean to offend you, but I can see how I came across a little prideful with my actions. Actually, I think I did mean to offend you. I think I was so full of adoration for my motor and myself that if anyone didn't acknowledge its significance, I probably made them feel inadequate on purpose.

"I have never thought about that before—the reasons why I made people feel that way. I guess I used the passive-aggressive quips as a defense. I've been on this River a long time. I have learned so many lessons that have just faded away. I was given the great gift of that motor. I was given the motor to bless other people, to help others. I felt special and unique. The more I used the motor to support myself, the less I used it for the intended purpose, which was to support others. It became a great sense of pride, and right about now I can't even remember one reason why I would be found worthy of this gift. Why was I given it in the first place? I used to be, well..." Self-Sufficient couldn't think of the word.

Immediately the word *reliant* came back to the forefront of Buddy's mind, and he spoke it out: "Reliant."

"Yes, Reliant," Self-Sufficient said, amazed that Buddy had said it out loud.

"I remember now that when I first met you, I saw that name on your canoe and thought maybe you stole it from someone named Reliant," Buddy said jokingly.

"That used to be my greatest gift, my greatest sense of pride," Reliant said, "that I was reliant on The Friend and The Guide for everything. I would wake up thinking Them for the new morning, seeking what They had in store for me that day. I would ask for guidance and wait for answers on everything. I was..." He looked down in despair, and then lifted his head and continued, "I want to be Reliant."

They both sat there, staring at The River, amazed at both the depth of the revelations and the fresh kindred spirit they felt for each other. It felt good to both of them to be on a road to reclaiming the truths they had learned at an earlier time but had so quickly forgotten.

CHAPTER 18

Dueling Natures

*"That which you feed will grow;
that which you starve will die."*
– Sir Common Sense

It was after some laughs, tears, and pure joy that Helper, Enough, and Courageous set out to continue in the work of Cheerful, finding those who were lost and helping set them free by the hand of The Friend. It wasn't long before they came across a group of people who had been set free of a great deception by Cheerful. They all had a sadness about them that was very apparent. The three gathered around them and began sharing stories of Cheerful and what she had done, what she had sacrificed. The group felt guilty that because of their deception, Cheerful was gone.

Enough spoke up. "Cheerful would have done what she did a hundred times over in order to help just one of you come to know The Friend. She was committed to helping others see that The Friend is the only One who can truly help, the only One who knows The River and each person's destiny here. She was sure of it."

Enough then shared her struggles, her triumphs, and her understanding of The Friend. The three of them spent some time there, sharing and encouraging the group.

* * *

Buddy and Reliant sat for a long time by The River's edge, contemplating what they would do next. Buddy knew he had to speak to the group of Encouragers about his experiences, but felt he was supposed to stay here for a while.

Reliant spoke up. "Buddy, in my insecurity and need for approval, I brought many vulnerable people to your group of Encouragers. I need to speak the truth I've been reminded of here. I think it's right for you to go there too, back to the group to make things right, but maybe you need a little more time here alone."

Buddy was deep in thought but, after a long silence, he said, "I do need to speak to them, and I do need to be here for a little while longer. I'll meet you there shortly. Thank you for coming to look for me and for being a friend."

Reliant patted Buddy on the shoulder and set off to the group of Encouragers.

As Buddy remained there, thinking about all the mistakes he'd made, he seriously wondered if he would ever be free of this dueling nature inside of him. Could he just do the right thing, or would he be forever riding a roller coaster of failures and successes? He felt discouraged, like maybe it would be better if he was on his own, so that his failures would only affect him and no one else. Anyway, he was much more comfortable alone.

He heard someone coming from the woods and got startled again. Thinking that Reliant had come back for something, he didn't even turn around and he said, "That was quick—you missed me that much?"

To Buddy's surprise, it wasn't Reliant, but someone else. He was holding some food and wood, apparently for a fire. Buddy was a little chilly and kind of hungry, so he hoped he would be invited to participate. He stood up and introduced himself, hoping to learn the person's name. "Hey, I'm Buddy. I just stopped here for a little while. I hope that's okay."

Buddy looked at the stranger, awaiting a response.

"Yeah, sure, Buddy, I come here from time to time too. I get to meet a bunch of people, share some stories and move on. Stay as long as you like."

Buddy nodded in thanks. "I didn't catch your name," he quickly shot back.

"I don't much like names, Buddy. I'm more of a being without labels or titles. I don't like people judging me by what they first hear or see or have been told about me. I'm a friend."

Buddy didn't seem to know this person, but he felt a little uncomfortable around him. He listened as the stranger told him all about the lies people believe and how so many people get caught up in one singular way to navigate The River.

"How is it that we can only follow one plan? There are so many people, so many differences among them. Everyone is unique; how can there be only one way? Doesn't seem to make sense with everything I see around me.

"I agree that everyone needs something to follow, some direction and guidance, but that stuff is for the weak. You don't strike me as someone who's weak, Buddy. You strike me as someone who's learned some valuable lessons and has some bruises to show for it. One way—seems kind of primitive, doesn't it?"

Buddy listened and thought a lot about what he was saying. It felt as though he was being lured into some sort of relative logic through compliments and a sense of piety. This didn't seem to click with what he had been told when he first came on The River. There was something inviting about what was being said, but nonetheless it didn't sit right within him. It had some logic, but it seemed a little familiar. Buddy thought more about what he had said and asked,

"What about truth? What determines what's true?"

"Truth," the guy said, "is what you determine it is. Why does your truth have to reconcile with my truth? We're all here finding our own way. We're doing the best we can, and each of our personalities, past experiences, and life lessons dictate what truth is for us. And to those truths we must remain committed."

Buddy thought how made-up and simple this theory—made out to be sophisticated—seemed to him.

The stranger looked at Buddy and could see that he was not getting through. "Well, Buddy, maybe I was wrong. You may need the simple truths of life, and possibly sometime in the future you'll be ready for the liberation that comes from this belief. No rules, no one telling you what truth is—true freedom. That Book you read talks about milk versus solid food. [24] It says the solid food is for the mature, and the guy writing it was saying he was amazed that they had not moved on to solid food yet but were still using milk, like an infant. I guess some people are never ready for the meat. Best of luck, Buddy."

As the stranger walked away, Buddy saw him slip back into the woods and he sort of reminded him of The Deceiver. *That's it*, Buddy thought, *he reminds me of The Deceiver*. Buddy was now a little more confused, but glad that individual was gone. He seemed like he knew

---

24 Hebrews 5:12-14, 1 Corinthians 3:2 NASB

what he was talking about, and had even referenced The Book. Buddy sat alone for a while, thinking about these things.

While his mind was going in continuous circles, he heard another noise coming from the woods. *What now?* he thought. *Is this Grand Central Station? I was hoping to be alone.*

Without looking at Buddy, The Friend walked past him and said gently, "Should I leave? Would you rather be alone?"

"I, um, I didn't know..." Before Buddy could finish, The Friend put His hand on his shoulder and said, "I know, Buddy. I'm just having a little fun with you. I can see that you may need some assistance with your conflicting thoughts. There is so much I'd love to tell you right now, but for today I'm going to stick to a few things."

Just as when The Voice had spoken to Buddy on the beach the first day on The River, Buddy perked up and was extremely eager to hear what was about to come out of his Friend's mouth.

The Friend sat down across from him and began with this: "There is always a natural fight within yourself. This fight is between two natures. One desires to be gratified, entertained, and safe. The other desires to be involved in a perfect destiny, no matter what the cost. As you can imagine, these two natures are constantly in opposition with each other. They have opposing goals that rarely, if ever, intersect or share any commonality. They are in direct opposition. The Book talks a lot about this, and I would like you to read these two sections right now."[25]

The Friend got up and walked down by The River to give Buddy some space to spend time reading. Buddy began reading and looked up for a moment to think, and noticed someone come rushing up to The Friend, looking panicked and worried.

Buddy lost focus on what he was doing and became fixated on what was going on by The River. He noticed The Friend comforting someone and then sending her off. As she was leaving, he saw that it was Helper. She left as quickly as she had come, and Buddy became worried and concerned. He wanted to be involved in what was going on. Immediately Buddy got up, left The Book, and trotted over to The Friend.

"What can I do?" Buddy blurted out to The Friend.

"About what, Buddy?"

"I want to help. Whatever Helper needs, I'm here. She looked worried," Buddy said, now also a little panicked.

"Buddy, do you think I am in control here? Do you feel like I am incapable of taking care of things? By you asking to help, you're rejecting the one thing I asked you to do. You're distracted because you want to assist

25 Galatians chapter 5, Romans chapters 7, 8

Helper. I understand that she plays a special part in your life, and maybe even will in the future. But right now, you've been sidetracked and are allowing your selfish nature to take control, being diverted to *do*, rather than to just *be*.

"I asked you directly to read some truths that you need to understand and absorb into your life. These truths will guide you to intimacy with Me, to help you become a stable force for good. They will also help you to not be ineffective and weak in your life. Do you think I cannot sustain this place without you? Do you trust Me, or your instinct? Decide right now, Buddy. You may not have all the clarity or information that you deem necessary, but this is a big question Buddy. Will you trust Me?"

Buddy felt kind of stupid and a little insignificant at that moment. Why couldn't he just have obeyed and sat and read, and minded his own business? He began to think about the question. Could he trust The Friend? He thought back to the mess he'd made and all the people he'd hurt in the last weeks, months, and years. He knew the answer; he knew he was tired of only trusting himself.

"Yes, I trust You."

"Thank you, Buddy. I won't lead you astray. Stay with Me, and in Me and you'll be okay. I love the fact that you're choosing to trust Me, Buddy. We've got a long, tiring, joyous, sorrowful, successful journey filled with failures, lessons, and friendship ahead together. It's where you're meant to be."

And it was at that moment that Buddy knew this was where he wanted to dwell, forever.

He began to backpedal and sat back down by The Book. He continued reading the specific passages, all the while thinking how immediately applicable and relevant the passages were.

The Friend gave Buddy a little time to continue reading and contemplating. Eventually, He came back and sat down across from Buddy.

"For as long as you are on this River, you will have two competing natures inside of you. The more you listen to one over the other, the greater it becomes. The more you feed the one over the other, the stronger it becomes. The more you neglect one over the other, the more it becomes insignificant and obsolete.

"Feed your spirit with truth. What you're reading is truth. This is why I gave you this Book the first day on The River. It will serve as a great source of truth, comfort, discipline, encouragement, and so many other things, if you read it and heed it. This is feeding your soul with exactly what you need, exactly when you need it. This is the only book like it in history, because it's living.

"You also read about freedom. You have been set free from the bondage of the fleshly and sinful nature. You once were bound by it, but I gave you freedom from it. You also read that you shouldn't turn that freedom into an opportunity for the fleshly desires to just do what they want. This freedom is not to just say 'no' to the bad things that hurt you, but 'yes' to the good things that free you. There are fruits that come from dwelling in the truth:[26] love, joy, peace, patience, kindness, goodness, faithfulness, gentleness, self-control.

"Let these reign in you, Buddy, because if these don't reign, then the opposition will. You will be filled with things that seem true, but are not: hate, sorrow, anxiousness, impatience, mean-spiritedness, falsehoods, faithlessness, and pride. You get to choose; I allow you the choice, but with that choice come consequences. I know that you've chosen the light, so make sure you feed that light so it will grow."

The Friend stood up, looking into the woods behind Buddy, and began once more, "You had an encounter recently with someone who seemed to be wise, at least in their own eyes. They quoted some passages from The Book but used them to prove their own theory. They used a truth and manipulated it to make what they were saying seem true. The milk and solid food are about spiritual truth, not about a relative truth that has no

26 Galatians 5:22-23 NASB

parameters. The milk is some of the elementary things I've taught you, like the fact that I'm in control and have made it possible for you to live rightly and follow My plan. Those are basic but important truths. The meat is getting deeper in your faith and living those truths out to the best of your ability. It's not just knowing the fundamentals, but it's practicing them and making an impact on The River for Me, for Truth, every day, even on the days you don't 'feel' like it. Usually that's when the truth you live has the greatest impact."

The Friend stopped and stared at Buddy, looking deep into his soul. Buddy looked right at The Friend and in that moment felt an awe—an awe that One so great could care so much about one so insignificant. An awe that there was a constant flow of wisdom and truth from within The Friend.

Buddy began to feel insignificant and unworthy, and he started thinking about all the things that had made him inadequate.

Right then, The Friend said, "Buddy, you are enough. Because you are with Me. Remember, you're enough. I love you, and because of that, you are enough."

Buddy had such peace come over him every time The Friend said that he was enough. A deep feeling grew inside him to want to please his Friend, but *Friend?* Buddy thought. *Is that the right name? Self-Sufficient could be a friend; Helper could be a special friend; but how could I call Him Friend?*

He felt deeply moved and had the feeling that some sort of revelation was about to make its way to the forefront of his mind.

"Buddy, I know what you're feeling, and I love where you are right now. Those who have this understanding of Me call Me Lord. I am so many things. One name could not capture My fullness, but for now, call Me Lord. That will help you remember that I am set apart, holy, and in control. I'm so proud of you, Buddy."

With that, The Lord motioned for Buddy to come over to The River's edge. As he stood next to The Lord, both staring out at The River, The Lord said, "Buddy, you have a full destiny with Me. You are going to impact so many lives on this River. You will encounter miracles, heartaches, and unspeakable joys.

"However, for now I need you to know Me and My way better. I am leaving you here for a while to meditate on My Words in The Book. I want you to dig deep, and read from start to finish the entire Book. I want you to see how everything fits together into one cohesive story. I want you to witness My love, joy, wrath, judgment, hope, sacrifice, and mercy through this Book.

"Only through reading it in its entirety can you grasp the big picture that helps you keep everything in true focus. So, stay, read, and watch yourself be healed and made ready for the tasks I will put before you. I'm proud of you, Buddy."

And with those words, his Lord walked away into the distance.

CHAPTER 19

Refreshing

"Of all spiritual disciplines prayer is the most central, because it ushers us into perpetual communion with the Father."
– Richard J. Foster

As Buddy sat alone in the little cove by The River, he held The Book in his hand and thought how large it looked. He wondered how long it would take to read through. Surely, He couldn't have literally meant to read the whole thing. He quickly found himself making excuses and thinking of reasons why he shouldn't take the time to read the whole thing right now. Maybe he could read bits and pieces at a time and work through it in a few months, or maybe even a year.

Then he heard a soft Voice in his head as he remembered what his Lord had said, "So stay, read, and watch yourself be healed, made ready for the tasks I will put before you."

He then resisted the other voices in his head and decided to trust what The Lord had said. He was ready for some healing and began to get excited about spending the time doing this. He began to anticipate what would happen and what lay before him.

Buddy spent the next few days reading, praying, and learning about this Book. He took small breaks, went for a walk, made a fire, and gathered some food while he gathered his thoughts. He took that time to think about what he read, remembering how what he had just gone through fit into what he had read days before.

The more he read, the more things made sense in their intended context. He anticipated the next portion of reading, awaiting what would come, what the next piece of the puzzle would be. As he read the second half of The Book, he realized that the anticipation that had built in The Book was all about his Friend, whom he now called Lord. He grew in his admiration, respect, love, and fear of The Lord. He felt so fortunate to have the opportunity to know Him so personally. He thought, *How could One so influential and significant care about me? How could One so perfect have the patience for one so imperfect and full of flaws?*

Once Buddy had finished The Book, he sat in awe of how all things revolved around The Lord, everywhere. It brought Buddy to a place of reassessing everything. He thought about his life before The River, what lay ahead, and all the mistakes he'd made. He was so inspired by what he had read that he vowed to dedicate everything to his Lord, trying to please The Lord, to be a friend, showing love and living what The Book had revealed to him.

One thing that was very apparent to him was the stark contrast between those who lived with The Lord and those who lived without Him. Between those who trusted in The Lord and those who tried to treat Him as just a good luck charm. He wanted to make sure he always kept The Lord in the highest position in his heart and head.

He was filled with passion and vigor to tell all those on The River what he'd just learned. But he knew that his time meditating, praying, and learning on his own had not yet come to an end.

* * *

Buddy spent what seemed like a minute, but was really a few more weeks, dedicating his time to getting to know The Book and The Lord better. He was also trying to include The Guide in his life as much as possible, seeing the presence of The Guide as the ultimate Gift from above. The more time he spent alone here, the more tuned in he felt with The Lord, The Guide, and The River. His heart and desire to help others on The River grew with each moment he spent alone in that cove.

Each day for Buddy consisted of waking up and reading a portion of The Book, meditating on it, and seeing how it could apply to his own life. He took walks, praying (now, praying was simply talking with The Lord, not seeing Him physically but knowing He was there) and trying to be led by The Guide.

He began to establish a routine for the days ahead when he would not be alone at the cove. He wrote down a system that would allow him to maintain this unity with The Lord, whether things were easy or difficult. Happy, sick, or healthy, no matter what the situation, this would help him to maintain this union, regardless of the outside influences that surrounded him.

As long as he could uphold this relationship, he could assure growth and greater faith.

On the days he forgot or was too busy, for whatever reason, to take the time to spend with The Lord, he didn't let it condemn him, but he received the grace given by The Lord to start fresh. Buddy had his own system for trying to maintain this relationship, and he thought he should copy it and give it to everyone he met. That way, they too could have a system for securing their walk with The Lord.

But then Buddy heard The Guide speaking in his mind. The Guide was clear, and through that still, small voice told him that his list was just for him, not for the rest of the world. He was told that a list like this could quickly become a system, and that system could quickly become an empty routine or a hollow tradition. His list, Buddy was told, was born out of experiences—both good and bad, and some good times and some hard trials—but they were *his* experiences. That list highlighted some things that Buddy needed to focus on.

The Guide told Buddy that this list would transform over time, emphasizing whatever he needed to focus on at the moment. Buddy realized the importance of everyone creating their own list from their experiences, so that the list did not become a meaningless process.

Although each of these steps for Buddy seemed important, practicing the presence of The Lord seemed to bring the most fruit and gave him the most peace. The premise for this practice was from a monk in the seventeenth century who every day, and in everything he did, always remembered that The Lord was with him.[27] No matter what he did, from the most menial task to the most important job, he did it as if it was The Lord asking him to do it. Everywhere he was, he remembered that The Lord was with him.

Doing this was difficult at first for Buddy, but the more he practiced it, the more natural it became. Soon enough, he not only believed but knew that his Lord was with him, all the time. This changed nominal, bor-

27 Brother Lawrence, *Practice of the Presence of God* (New Kensington, PA: Whitaker House, 1982); original published in French in 1692.

ing situations into opportunities that he would have never seen before this practice. This practice was by far the most life-changing for him.

CHAPTER 20

Out and About

"Christ-likeness is your eventual destination, but your journey will last a lifetime."
– Rick Warren

Buddy woke up one morning, beginning his routine that he had faithfully done so many mornings before. As he began praying he thought about Helper, and about Enough, Cheerful, Self-Sufficient, and Courageous. His heart went out to them, wondering where they were and what they were doing. He felt prompted that the time was near to venture out—to leave his little cove and start making an impact on The River. But he knew he would need to come back here periodically to regain his focus and intimacy with The Lord and The Guide.

As Buddy finished his morning rituals, he began thinking about Sorrowful. He began thinking about all the hurt, pain, and suffering she had endured in her past, and how he had just left her there. He felt his heart hurt for her and for all that she'd been through. She was so loyal, and Buddy had left her there alone to manage everything.

He became overwhelmed with guilt and remorse for what he had done. Immediately Buddy got on his knees and began praying and asking forgiveness for the wrong he had done, and for an opportunity to make it right. He prayed for a while and knew what he was being called to do. As he prayed, he kept hearing the word *precious*. Not sure what it was about, he got up and walked back over to the fire pit.

Buddy packed his stuff into his canoe and set off to the Cove of the Encouragers to find Sorrowful and those who had gathered there. He couldn't say for sure how long he had been gone, but he knew it was a long time. He began to worry, and then immediately remembered that he needed to replace that fear with truth. There is therefore now no condemnation for those who are in The Lord.[28] He kept repeating that to himself and remembered that he could combat any fleshly thought by walking in the Spirit of The Lord and thinking about things that bring life and peace. He would not think about the mistakes he'd made, but about the restoration and life that would come from what The Lord could do through any situation and any failure.

---

28 Romans 8:1 ESV

He began thinking about what it would be like to talk to Sorrowful and to bring her the truth about The Lord and about herself. Buddy began to smile, thinking about such things.

* * *

As Buddy rounded a corner, to his amazement there were what seemed like hundreds of people occupying this Cove of the Encouragers. He began scanning the horizon and all he could see were people. They had even cleared out the cove to make more room for greater numbers of people.

He wondered if Sorrowful was even there anymore. As he ran his canoe up onto the shore, he was greeted by a seriously happy couple of people. They gave Buddy a hug and welcomed him to the Cove of the Encouragers. He would have never believed that so many people would have come to this place. As he walked through the camps of people, he came to the shrine to Cheerful and noticed that hundreds of people had laid flowers, gifts, and other things at the foot of the shrine. He felt that what he had done out of an earnest desire to remember Cheerful had been cheapened and made out to be an idol, or a crutch for people who just needed to meet The Friend to find true encouragement.

The longer he was there, the more it seemed that people were forcing themselves and others to be encouraging, for no other reason than because it made them temporarily feel special and satisfied.

As he was noticing the shallowness of the actions of all the people around him, Sorrowful showed up, gave him a big punch in the arm in jest, and said, "Welcome back, Chief."

"Chief, eh?" Buddy said, not knowing what to say to her since he had left rather abruptly.

"So, you decided to come back and grace us with your presence?"

Buddy could tell that Sorrowful was being sarcastic because he had obviously hurt her. She kept looking in his eyes for longer than normal glances, probably hoping for an explanation or apology. She looked tired, skinnier than he remembered, and just worn.

"Can we take a walk?" Buddy asked politely. He looked at Sorrowful, waiting for a reply.

Trying to seem quasi-uninterested, Sorrowful said, "There's a lot going on today, so we need to be quick."

Buddy didn't take offense but remembered why he was here. Suddenly, the word from when he was praying a few days ago came into his mind: *precious*. He started walking and thinking about how to begin. Again, that word came into his mind—*precious*.

Buddy decided not to think, but instead trusted that The Guide was telling him something substantial and timely.

"You are precious," was all he said, all he was able to say.

"What did you say?" Sorrowful asked snappily, almost sounding offended.

"I said, you are precious. Well, actually someone told me you were precious."

Then all the thoughts he had about her became clear, intentional, relatable thoughts in his head that he knew he had to speak. So, Buddy continued to tell Sorrowful of his experience at his other cove.

"Over the past few weeks and months, I've been thinking a lot about you. I kept going back to some of our initial conversations, and I remembered that you've had it tough so far in life, that you probably have a difficult time trusting people. And here I left you alone to fend for yourself. For that, I'm deeply sorry. But I am here to tell you that you are not hidden, or hopeless. There has been Someone all along who heard your cries for help, and even though you don't think anyone heard you, He did. He wept at the things that happened to you and still holds a place of deep affection for you in His heart."

Buddy stared at Sorrowful, and thoughts came into his head that were not his—things to say that he felt uncomfortable saying. After all, Buddy had not been through these things; he had not witnessed what had happened to Sorrowful. Who was he to say these things? As these thoughts raced through his head, Sorrowful looked up with tears pouring down her cheeks, saying, "What else?"

Buddy became emboldened, filled with compassion and courage, and spoke what was in his mind. "You can't even imagine how many other people of all ages and sexes, all races and backgrounds have been abused and left alone, used, and discarded. You will, in time, be a beacon for the One who loves them and has seen *everything*. As He wants to be your refuge and sanctuary, so too are there millions still in those situations who need rescuing and liberation. You are Precious, and you will be with One who adores you forever. He's calling you by name, Precious. He's calling you to know Him and to be restored."

Precious began to feel overwhelmed and wept uncontrollably. As she abandoned all dignity and pride, letting go, she wept greatly, asking Buddy, "What have I done to deserve such affection?"

Buddy didn't know what to do but to rub her back and be silent. As he looked up across The River, he saw The Lord standing on the opposite side, waving to send Precious to Him.

Buddy softly spoke to Precious, "He's there." Buddy pointed in the direction of The Lord and told her that He was waiting for her.

As Buddy looked back down, Precious was already waist deep in the water, wading through it frantically to get to The Lord. He watched her with tears running down his face as she made it across.

As she stood before Him, at first she sheepishly looked at Him, but listened to what He said to her with great interest. Buddy saw The Lord speaking tenderly to Precious, with one hand on each shoulder as He gazed into her eyes, her soul. They wept together for a long time. Then, to his surprise, he saw Precious wading back across The River toward him and he thought, That was quick.

Soaking wet, she walked up to Buddy, hugged him, and said, still weeping, "Buddy, you're Magnificent." That was all she said as she stared into his eyes. She was silent as she stared, and then she waded back across The River to Magnificent's Lord.

When she was halfway across The River, she looked back and said, "Take care of these people and share what you shared with me—they all need it. I'll be back after I take care of some business!"

* * *

Buddy's heart and mind were full. He would not have traded this experience for any of the situations, smells, or feelings that he had wanted to bottle up previously. This was living on The River as it was meant to be. As Buddy made his way back to the cove, he thought about what lay ahead and all the things he might encounter. He had a feeling of anticipation—no fear, no apprehension, just a new sense of purpose and a skip in his step. He thought again about Helper and how he wished he could share with her everything that had happened.

Strange, he thought, *that would usually be something I would want to share with my sisters.* He knew in his heart that his time with Helper was not over, by any means. Questions began to pop into his mind about things he'd never thought of before: *Could I ever lose the love and attention of The Lord? Is this River the end, or is there something more? Why are there so many people who claim to follow The Lord but still seem sad and without hope? Will I ever see Cheerful again?*

Great questions that needed attention, but that was for another day. For now, Buddy was tired yet full, content, and confident. Once again, his eyes became heavy as he sat down under a shady tree. Buddy had drifted off into a peaceful sleep when he was suddenly awakened by a Voice: "Buddy, it's time to wake up."

Characters

Buddy – the man on The River of Life

The Guide – the Holy Spirit

The Voice who becomes The Friend, then The Lord
    – Jesus

The Creator – God the Father

The Book/The Great Book – the Bible

The Deceiver/The Destroyer/Shadowy Figure – Satan

The Gift – Eternal life, reconciliation to God through
    Jesus

Canoe Seeker, Self-Sufficient, Striver, Helper,
    Disappointed, Excited, Sorrowful – fellow travelers
    Buddy meets along The River

Cheerful, Funny, and Smart are Buddy's sisters
Cheerful remains Cheerful
Funny's name changes to Enough
Smart's name becomes Courageous

The Waterfall – represents heaven, or the transition
    from this life to the next

About the Author

Born and raised on Long Island in New York, Andrew has been chasing truth and the Author of Truth his whole life. This book reflects that search. Andrew has a bachelor's degree in theology, a master's degree in business, and has taught with the global missionary organization Youth With A Mission in America, Europe, Africa, Australia, and Asia. During this time, he has focused more and more on knowing God's Word as a means to knowing God.

In 2010, he created a program to facilitate reading the entire Bible in eight days. The idea is that in reading the Book as a whole, one experiences the continuous heart of God. The God of the Old Testament is the God of the New Testament. One book opens your eyes to the other as God's plan for His people stretches across testaments and time.

Seeing God in the big picture has so impacted Andrew that he has led hundreds of others on "Bible weeks," where they too experience the Bible in one unbroken story of God and us. This book is another way in which Andrew is pointing us to our need to know God's Word—to keep going no matter the cost, pain, or disappointments life throws at us.

Along with his passion for the Bible, Andrew is extremely fond of his wife, six children, dog, cookies, mint chocolate chip ice cream, and shoes.

For more information on Bible seminars and Bible reading weeks:

www.thewordjourney.com
info@thewordjourney.com